Racism, Sexism and Homophobism: Managing Harassment in the Workplace

Second Printing

BY

CROSS CULTURAL COMMUNICATIONS INTERNATIONAL, INC.

WINNIPEG, MANITOBA, CANADA

1994

Racism, Sexism, Homophobism: Managing Harassment in the Workplace

Cross Cultural Communications International, Inc.

Winnipeg, Manitoba, Canada

ISBN 1-895631-07-6

ATTENTION!

Publications by

Cross Cultural Communications International, Inc.

- Interviewing Aboriginal Peoples
- The McDonald Guide to Aboriginal Issues Today
- The McDonald Guide to Aboriginal Issues Today: Teacher's Guide
- The McDonald Guide to Employment Equity: Designated Group Retention
- The McDonald Guide to Managing Diversity
- Guide de la gestion de la diversité
- The McDonald Guide to Communicating Across Cultures
- The McDonald Quarterly Report
- Racism, Sexism and Homophobism: Managing Harassment in the Workplace

Table of Contents

Part One
Self-Examination Questionnaire

Part One: Self-Examination Questionnaire

Directions:

Read each of the following questions and circle the answer, or answers, which you believe to be the most appropriate. Check your answers with those given at the end of the section. The references in the answer key on page 9 will direct you to the relevant section of the manual.

1. If a woman has just received flowers from someone whom she felt was beginning to harass her, what would you recommend as the best course of action she take? She should:

   a) give the flowers back to the sender.
   b) throw the flowers in the garbage.
   c) give the flowers away to someone who would appreciate them.
   d) return them to the florist.

2. A black man has been subjected to racial jokes in the workplace from several colleagues. What should he do first? He should:

   a) call the Human Rights Commission and lay a complaint.
   b) write a letter to the management of the company.
   c) approach the 'jokers' and inform them that he does not appreciate their 'humour'.
   d) inform his supervisor about the situation.

3. An Asian manager received a transfer to another office. The manager sensed resentment on the part of one of the employees. Later, the employee asked the manager, "How did you get this job?". He should:

a) treat the question as innocent; the person is just curious. Answer the question.
b) suspect that there are hidden motives to the question, such as determining whether he has the 'necessary' qualifications for the position. He should not answer the question. He should fire the person.
c) answer the question, but will do so only to all the staff and give a little talk on how minority managers face perceptions that they get jobs for which they are not qualified.
d) do the same as above, but fire the person who asked the question, on the grounds of racist attitudes.

4. It is not possible to harass unintentionally. TRUE OR FALSE?

5. Which statements below are true to the concept of prejudice.

a) It is learned from persons of influence.
b) People are born with prejudices.
c) Some people like to blame others for their troubles.
d) Some people believe that their culture is superior to other cultures.

6. Which of the following is not harassment:

a) telling jokes which ridicule the cultural/racial background of an employee in the workplace.
b) denying an employee a promotion due to gender, culture, race, religion or place of national origin.
c) displaying photographs which depict women without any clothing.
d) tying a promotion or benefits to sexual favours.

7. A potential business partner from South Asia has invited you over for a home cooked meal. You suspect that the partner may be attracted to you, but you are not interested. Yet you want to maintain good business relations. You should:

a) politely decline, but encourage further business meetings at the office.
b) accept, but make sure that the message gets across that you are not interested.
c) accept and not say anything about the suspected attraction.
d) decline, and openly state the reason why.

8. In a recent study, what percentage of female executives in the United States said that they either experienced, or knew of someone who had experienced, sexual harassment?

a) 12%
b) 53%
c) 35%
d) 61%

9. Which of the following are true when developing a harassment policy.

a) the policy should define clearly what constitutes harassment.
b) the policy should not be specific about penalties for harassment because harassment has a wide range of actions.
c) there is no federal or provincial legislation concerning harassment.
d) the policy should contain a procedure for complaints to be reported, acted upon, and resolved.

10. Heterosexism is:

a) the belief that sex should be varied in content and practice.
b) to favour, rather than disfavour, women.
c) the belief that homosexuals are inferior.
d) the belief that heterosexuals are superior.

11. Once a harassment situation has been resolved with disciplinary action against the harasser, what tends to be the best strategy for a manager to re-establish a productive workplace?

a) ensure that the harasser and the victim have no contact with each other.
b) have the harasser personally apologize to the victim and all other staff for the behavior.
c) have the victim give a seminar on harassment.
d) use inter-group conflict resolution strategies.

12. Discrimination:

a) is an act of prejudice.
b) is always a result of prejudice.
c) does not include harassment.
d) is the same as racism.

13. One of the pieces of evidence in a harassment case is the statement by the harasser that the woman always stood very close to him when speaking to him. He indicated that "I am not racist, and therefore I pursued her regardless of her being from Chile." Choose the most appropriate statement below.

a) the evidence should be considered in favour of the man. He thought she was making a pass at him.
b) the man should be disciplined fully according to the harassment policy for the type of harassment he committed.
c) the man and the woman may have just had a cultural misunderstanding. An informal discussion meeting should clear up the misunderstanding.
d) anyone who stands too close to other people should not be able to charge others with harassment.

14. Can a manager who fails to adequately act upon a harassment complaint be charged himself/herself?

Yes or No

15. Which of the following statements do not indicate gender bias?

a) She's not at her desk. She must be in the Ladies' room.
b) She got a raw deal. Did she cry?
c) The boss critiqued her performance. She'll be terribly upset.
d) She's having another child. She'll need a raise.

16. Which below is the ideal first step for a victim of harassment to take:

a) inform the manager as soon as possible.
b) talk to a friend or colleague about the situation.
c) confront the harasser. Inform him/her of your feelings regarding their actions.
d) approach the local human rights commission with a complaint.

ANSWER AND REFERENCE KEY		
1.	d	SEE PART V SECTION A
2.	c or d	SEE PART V SECTION A
3.	c	SEE PART III SECTION A
4.	False	SEE PART IV
5.	a c d	SEE PART II SECTION A
6.	b	SEE PART III
7.	c	SEE PART IV SECTION F
8.	b	SEE PART IV SECTION E
9.	a, d	SEE PART V SECTION C
10.	c d	SEE PART II SECTION C
11.	d	SEE PART V SECTION B
12.	a	SEE PART II SECTION B
13.	c	SEE PART IV SECTION F
14.	Yes	SEE PART V SECTION B
15.	d	SEE PART IV SECTION F
16.	c	SEE PART V SECTION A

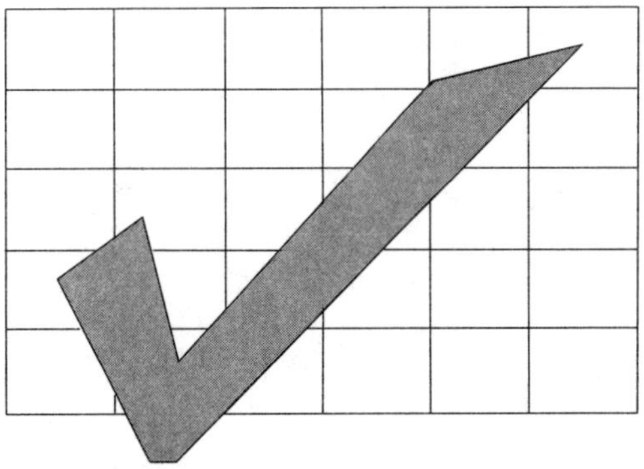

Part Two

What is Harassment?

Practical Definitions

Part Two: What is Harassment? Practical Definitions

The recent Clarence Thomas Senate hearings in the United States focussed the public eye on sexual harassment in the workplace. While sexual harassment is the most frequently discussed type of harassment, few have addressed other less frequent forms of harassment in the workplace. Also, while many have addressed harassment in its concrete visible forms, few have delved into the **real causes of harassment**: **prejudice and discrimination**.

While women have suffered the brunt of harassment in the workplace, they are not alone in being the victims. Ethnic minorities, persons with disabilities, the aged and the homosexual (to name a few groups) have also been subject to harassment.

The issue of harassment has been addressed by a number of organizations, including provincial human rights commissions, the Canadian Human Rights Commission, and many private corporations. Below is the most comprehensive and precise definition of harassment that can be found:

Harassment means any unwelcome behaviour, typically repetitive in nature, which denies individuals their dignity and respect and which is offensive, embarrassing and humiliating.

While the area of harassment can be very ambiguous, a guideline to follow is that any behaviour which is considered **unwelcome** might be considered harassment. **Harassment is in the eye of the beholder.**

The law forbids discrimination on prohibited grounds including all those actions which are based on prejudiced attitudes.

A. PREJUDICE

Prejudice is the habit of prejudging groups or individuals, on the basis of real or imagined cultural and/or racial characteristics. It is usually a negative prejudgment of others formed prior to adequate experience with that group or individual. **It is a learned attitude**.

Foremost, prejudice is an attitude. It is a thought, attitude or feeling that judges all members of a certain group. It takes many forms such as prejudice towards racial minorities, women, homosexuals, and those who carry the AIDS virus. **People are not born with prejudices. They are usually taught prejudice** by someone in authority whom they trust, such as parents.

While not all prejudices are negative, most prejudices regarding minorities are negative. When individuals are asked to describe their attitudes toward a minority group, negative attitudes are recorded ten times more often than positive ones.

Stereotypes express prejudice because they reflect the belief that all members of a group have the same characteristics. For example, "All blacks are musical" or "All Jews are wealthy".

Prejudice and stereotyping can be difficult to avoid and even the best-intentioned can make errors. Prejudicial stereotypes can lead to discriminatory or differential treatment based on the assumptions expressed.

There are several causes of prejudiced attitudes.

* **Scapegoating**: Some individuals when they experience frustration in their lives which they are unable to account for, look for individuals or groups whom they believe are responsible for the frustration; 'a scapegoat' to blame for their troubles. They search for reasons why some one, or some group, is responsible for the problems which they are experiencing, other than themselves. For example, some people have claimed that there is a Jewish Business Conspiracy that is bent on the destruction of Christian society, and that this Jewish conspiracy has been laying off many Christians from jobs. These people want to believe that some group, other than themselves, is responsible for their frustration.

* **Defective personality**: Generally, those who scapegoat do so because they have a defective personality. Individuals who exhibit strong negative attitudes against particular groups generally have the strong anxieties and insecurities of neurotic people. They are afraid to take responsibility for themselves.

While the above may explain why prejudice occurs in individuals, it does not explain why communities as a whole, or societies such as in South Africa, may collectively hold prejudices against an ethnic group.

Ethnocentrism is the belief that one's own culture is superior to those of other groups.

* **Ethnocentrism**: almost entire societies can believe that it is justifiable to hold prejudices, and hence practice discrimination against members of another group. Stereotypes reinforce ethnocentrism to some degree. Stereotypes, however, can also work positively for particular groups. For example, by portraying all police officers as being mainstream male Canadians, mainstream male Canadians receive an advantage when they apply for positions as police officers.

* **Belief in Inherent Characteristics**: many Canadians believe, in spite of evidence to the contrary, that individuals inherit behavioural, cultural and psychological characteristics along with the colour of hair, skin and eyes. For example: "All Chinese are intelligent!".

* **Economic Competition**: the belief that another group is an economic threat can lead to prejudice and discrimination. Mainstream Canadians may feel threatened by the presence of minorities in the workforce and by personnel policies supportive of minorities, for example, "All you have to do to get ahead these days is to be a disabled aboriginal woman!"

  In a similar vein, missionaries in the colonial days of North America maintained that aboriginal people were incapable of taking care of themselves in a modern society and should therefore be taken care of by the church. This rationalization was used many times to limit the economic competitiveness of aboriginal people with mainstream immigrants and to bolster the prominence of the church in terms of monies and lands received from the government to care for the aboriginal people.

* **Tradition:** when things have always been done in a certain way, the tendency is to assume that "the way things have always been is the way things will and should always be." Tradition can lead to resistance and discrimination towards 'outsiders' or 'non-traditional' members of the workforce.

* **Visibility:** where prejudiced attitudes prevail, these are readily focussed on minority group members who are visibly distinguishable on the basis of race, ethnicity, religion, gender, or disability. Members of these minority groups are easy targets for discrimination.

Members of visible minority groups, aboriginal people and women, are often not represented or are underrepresented in advertisements, promotional materials, and among interviewers, recruiters and managers.

This absence of role models gives a subtle message to mainstream and minority Canadians that members of minority groups are insignificant outsiders in many Canadian organizations and in Canadian society in general.

Visible minorities, aboriginal Canadians and women who do not see fellow group members on recruitment and interviewing teams, in promotional materials or in managerial positions will perceive that they are unwelcome. In turn, this may result in lack of confidence or interest in trying for various positions.

The police sector has been notorious for its lack of opportunities for minority peoples. Many minority peoples (including women) express the belief that a career in policing would be without opportunities for promotion. Discrimination within the police force would ensure that they remain at the bottom. The **Ontario Race Relations and Policing Task Force** hearings confirmed the pervasiveness of the attitude expressed in a recent CBC Radio interview with a black youth who flatly dismissed the notion of a police career, saying:

> "If I became a police officer my boss is always going to be white."

B. DISCRIMINATION

Discrimination is behaviour which is usually rooted in prejudiced attitudes. Discrimination is an act of differential treatment toward an individual as a member of a group, or toward a group, which usually creates a disadvantage for that individual or group.

Prejudicial attitudes and beliefs lead to various discriminatory forms of behavior. Such acts of discrimination range across a wide spectrum of human behaviors:

* Verbal expression of prejudice in the form of jokes, expression of stereotypes, racial slurs, sexist comments, etc.

* Avoidance of social contact

* Discriminatory behavior that is actively detrimental to its intended or unintended victims

* Physical attacks

* Extermination: the killing of individuals or entire groups (genocide)

However, one does not need to be prejudiced in order to discriminate.

* an owner of a bar receives complaints from the regular clientele about the 'unwashed' who have lately been starting to frequent the bar. The owner is forced to choose between allowing the 'unwashed' in, or discriminating against them, regardless of the owner's own attitudes, in order to placate the regular clientele. In this situation, the owner is discriminating, but is not necessarily prejudiced. To the victim, however, the result is the same.

Harassment is considered a form of discriminatory behaviour. It is designed to disadvantage minority groups, including women.

Harassment is just a further degree of discrimination. It is an action which is blatantly based on a prejudice, and which disregards the rights of human beings. It must be remembered, therefore, that minorities are disadvantaged because of prejudice and discrimination. Should prejudiced attitudes and discriminatory acts be eliminated, then systemic discrimination would soon disappear as well.

Minority employees in the workplace often have a difficult time with prejudice. They believe that they must work twice as hard as mainstream employees to break down stereotypes about themselves, and achieve equal recognition for their contribution to the organization. When a minority person encounters harassment, it is often interpreted as a blatant message that he/she is not accepted in the workplace.

C. GROUNDS OF DISCRIMINATION

There are many groups that experience discrimination in Canadian society. The following is an examination of specific types of discrimination. All these areas are covered under the various Human Rights Codes. Below is a diagram detailing a few different types of discrimination which may be evident in the workplace and in society.

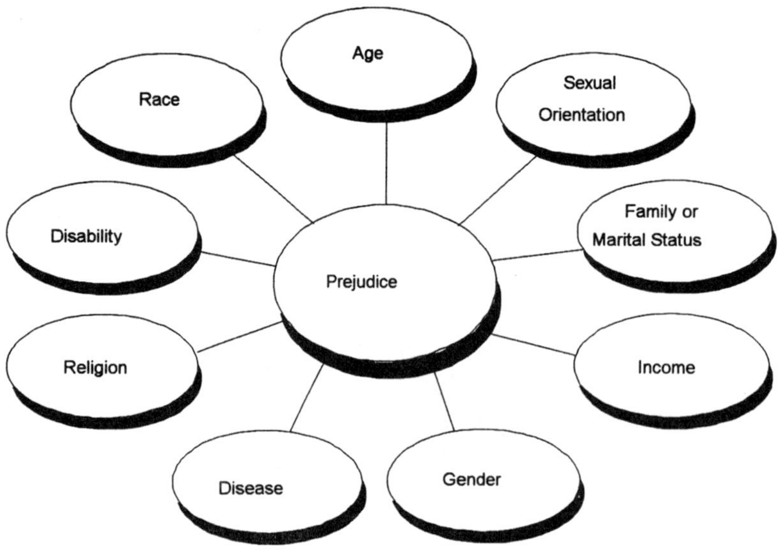

1. Gender

Women have not been accepted as equal to men in the Western world. They have not enjoyed the same political rights and economic freedoms that men have enjoyed. By virtue of their gender, women have even been denied equality with men. With changes in legislation, and with proactive government programs, such as employment equity and equal-pay-for-work-of-equal-value, women have been slowly achieving a relatively equal position in society. With that change must come changes in the culture of the workplace.

For the longest time, it was assumed that men would hold senior positions in the workplace. Women in the workplace were expected to assist men. It was in these circumstances that some men abused their positions of power and exploited women.

Sexism can be defined as any attitude, action, or institutional structure which, knowingly or systemically, subordinates a person on the basis of gender (male or female).

An individual may be expected to perform certain roles, due to his or her gender. For example, women may be expected to occupy secretarial positions in an office. It is very rare that a man occupy such a position.

In the same light, it is expected that women are unable to occupy certain roles in society. For example, people often do not perceive that women can be senior managers or executives. Some people have difficulty working under a woman because of their perceptions that women "should be at home with the children".

Some men may believe that their wives, while they may also be working at full-time positions, must take the responsibilities of house work and child care. Some believe that a woman's first priority is the home and that if she chooses to go to work full-time, then she must do so knowing that her responsibilities also continue to include the single responsibility for the condition of the home.

The harassment that many women face at the workplace, **sexual harassment**, is generally considered the most common due to the fact that there are many more women in the workforce, and in lower positions, than any other social minority. Sexual harassment, while it has existed for almost time immemorial, had only come to the public eye with civil rights legislation, and most recently, the allegations of Professor Anita Hill that Clarence Thomas had sexually harassed her.

Sexual harassment is any repeated unwelcome behaviour which is sexual in nature. It may involve a colleague repeatedly asking a worker to go out for dinner, or a manager who places conditions of sexual favours on job retention, promotions, and any other workplace activities. It can also be a colleague or manager who displays photographs which are perceived to be demeaning, embarrassing or offensive.

However, not all sexual harassment is perpetuated by men against women. There have been a few cases where women have sexually harassed men.

* A university student in a Canadian university was sexually harassed by his female professor.

There have also been situations documented where gay men and lesbians have been harassed by other gay men and lesbians. In addition, situations exist where women have sexually harassed gay men. These situations are indicative that sexual harassment is not limited to women as victims, although women have borne the brunt of the harassment.

Finally, some women in power positions have subjected other women to sexual harassment.

* A woman manager for a media organization sent a female researcher/reporter to a man from whom information was sought. The researcher/reporter later learned that she was sent as a 'gift'.

2. Family or Marital Status

Many women have been denied work on the basis that they are married. Some employers feel that a woman who has responsibilities at home will not be able to dedicate herself to a job as much as a man. Those employers believe that the woman might become pregnant so that they would have to hire someone else anyway to replace her while she is gone. A woman in this situation is being discriminated against on the basis of marital status.

* a woman has been taunted at the workplace by a colleague who has teased, "looking forward to seeing your husband?!". This woman believes there is no room for any references to her marital life in the workplace. This type of harassment may be based on person's marital status.

Some managers believe that a woman who has a family, i.e. children, will always be taking time off to take the children to a doctor and to stay home when a child is sick. A manager or colleague who chooses to make remarks, or deny the woman access to particular benefits or privileges, responsibilities or promotions, may be harassing on the basis of family status.

* A manager has said to a woman when she has asked for a sick day because her child is sick at school, "What is that kid's problem?! Do you realize how important it is to get this work done? I am seriously going to have to reconsider your position with us if this is going to keep interfering with your work! I took a chance on you when I hired you, wondering if you were going to be as committed to your job".

The woman above is being harassed on the basis of family status. The employer is clearly comparing her to a man; i.e. "as committed to your job".

3. Sexual Orientation

There is the perception that homosexuals are 'different' from other people. In some instances, that perception is that they are abnormal; that there is something wrong with them. Some may even consider that they are suffering from a disease.

Homophobism: The prejudice and discrimination directed towards gay men and lesbian women. Often, homophobia translates into blatant discrimination or violence against gay men and lesbian women.

As a result of the perceived differences, there are those who ignore the capabilities of the individual and focus on their 'difference'.

* An elementary school teacher in Manitoba has been refused positions at schools due to his sexual orientation, despite his obvious excellent qualifications and good record.

* The homosexual community has continuously been attacked in major Canadian cities by gangs of 'gay-bashers'. These gangs wander through communities where homosexuals are known to reside, and subsequently assault any men that they encounter. Members of the homosexual community have died under such circumstances.

* The Canadian Armed Forces has decided that while it will not dismiss homosexuals who have already entered the armed forces, due to the Charter of Rights and Freedoms, it will not hire any who identify themselves as such. It is well-known that homosexuals experience a great deal of harassment in the military.

Heterosexism: the belief that those who are heterosexual are superior. Heterosexism has generally relied on religious doctrine in upholding heterosexuality as superior.

While homophobism focuses on the sexual orientation of others, heterosexism focuses on one's own sexual orientation.

The homosexual community, unlike some other minority groups, is not a visible group. Unless individuals identify themselves as being gay, there is the possibility that many others in the workplace will not know that one of their colleagues is gay.

For this reason, the gay man or woman in the workplace may experience unintentional harassment where managers and colleagues may be making remarks or executing policies that may be insensitive or discriminatory towards the homosexual community without realizing that one of their co-workers is gay.

Due to the social stigma which has been attached to the homosexual community, i.e., abnormality, many gay men and women may hesitate to declare themselves as gay.

Today, one of the major issues facing the homosexual community is AIDS. This disease has ravaged the gay/lesbian community, though it has not limited its spread to them.

4. Disease

In the early 1980s, the spread of AIDS among the gay population in North America galvanized and labelled the community. Once the extent of the disease was known and the ramifications for both the homosexual and heterosexual communities were publicized, anyone who declared themselves to be gay was often considered to have AIDS.

I began to wonder when I started to attend funerals every week. I knew that something had to be going on.

Ignorance about the nature of the disease and the means by which it spreads and infects people caused almost mass hysteria towards anyone who is gay or anyone who has contracted the disease.

* Parents pulled their children from a school in the United States when it was learned that one of the students at the school was HIV positive.

* A man, who was sharing a booth on a train with a gay man, demanded that he be moved to another booth when he learned that the other man was gay. He also questioned the steward about the cleaning process used to clean the glass from which he was drinking. The man was afraid that he might catch AIDS because he was sitting beside someone who was gay.

In most cases, the AIDS in the workplace issue is one of discrimination, and not necessarily of harassment. Situations have occurred where individuals, because it may not have been possible to fire them once it is learned that they are HIV positive, have been harassed in order to induce them to leave the workplace.

While AIDS is not the only disease which provokes harassment, it is the most predominant.

5. Income

Discrimination on the basis of income is prohibited by many of the provincial Human Rights Codes. There is discrimination against those who earn more than others; whose family income and, therefore, lifestyle may tend to be at a somewhat higher level than the majority in the workplace; and discrimination against those who are poor or whose income falls much lower than others in the workplace.

* A woman was laid-off from her employment because it was perceived that her husband, a lawyer, could afford to take care of her.

Discrimination against those who are impoverished is much more prevalent. There are those who cannot afford the quality of clothing or the expensive lunches and coffee breaks which some in the workplace may take for granted.

* A poorer person was not considered for a promotion because it was perceived that she did not have the income needed to dress properly to meet clients.

Harassment of those with higher or lower incomes generally may entail "teasing" about either a fur coat or an old worn coat. It may entail "shaming" people about their level of income.

6. Age

Similarly, some people may believe that elderly people should not participate in the workforce, that they should vacate their jobs for younger people coming up the system and needing jobs or promotions.

There is the stereotype that older people would not be familiar with the 'changing culture', that they may be behind the times and unable to relate to changing values and circumstances of society.

* some organizations pressure some senior managers towards early retirement. Some also provide financial incentives for elderly employees to retire.

There are also those who believe that anyone who is young cannot have the experience and the knowledge to carry out a task or do a job as well as someone who is older. They believe that the person is "too green" as a result of their age.

* A non-profit community organization in a major Canadian city has elected a man in his late twenties to be their president. The man was elected despite his youth, as indicated in a newsletter article, and due to his exceptional abilities.

7. Race

There are a number of subcategories of Racism. Much of the Human Rights literature refers separately to ancestry, national origin, ethnic origin, and colour. These items can all be considered under the umbrella of prejudice on the basis of race.

Racism is any attitude, action or institutional structure which subordinates a person because of his or her colour or racial origin, perceived colour or racial origin, national (or perceived national) origin, and ethnic (or perceived ethnic) origin.

* To say that Black people are intellectually inferior to white people, and white people are intellectually inferior to oriental people, is racist.

* Blacks in Nova Scotia were not getting served in many bars in Halifax because of the colour of their skin. Their frustration resulted in a racial scene in the summer of 1991.

* When the management of a bar excludes certain groups because their regular clientele demand that they be refused service, they are still imposing racist policies although they may personally not hold racist attitudes towards those groups.

It can therefore be asserted that one does need to be prejudiced in order to discriminate.

With increasing immigration, primarily from non-traditional countries, the issue of racism is coming more to the forefront of key social issues. In addition, the resurgence of the Aboriginal Peoples has brought to the public's attention the role that racism has played in the near genocide of these peoples.

* The Aboriginal Justice Inquiry in Manitoba found that racism played a key role in the sixteen year delay to bring the killers of Helen Betty Osbourne, of The Pas Manitoba, to justice, although the community knew who had committed the crime within a few days.

* The Toronto Police Service is racked by allegations of racism because members have shot several Blacks in the past three years.

8. Religion

One of the values of North American society, and a key principle, is the guarantee of freedom of religion. Many immigrants came to North America to flee religious persecution in other countries, including Europe. Wars have been fought for the right of religious freedom. Hence, many of the Human Rights Codes prohibit discrimination on the basis of religion.

* One of the reasons that Canada sent soldiers to fight in the Second World War was to safeguard freedoms, including freedom of religion. Recently, some branches of the Royal Canadian Legion denied Sikhs their freedom of religion by prohibiting turbans in their Legion Hall.

Harassment on the basis of religion may include the demand that a Sikh with a turban remove his turban in order to receive service. Such a demand is demeaning to the individual, and involves an abuse of power.

9. Physical or Mental Disability

Persons with disabilities, both physical and mental, have suffered enormously from prejudice and discrimination. Often the attitudes are unintentional, stemming from ignorance of the issues affecting persons with disabilities.

* The chairman of the United States President's Council on Disability, who uses a wheelchair, was denied a seat on an airline because he could not walk on the plane.

* Mentally challenged individuals are often considered incapable of handling even the simplest tasks. Many people do not recognize that everyone has skills and abilities that can be utilized.

Those who have the most difficulty are those who fall into several of the disadvantaged categories. For example, aboriginal people who have disabilities may tend to experience greater barriers and difficulties. There are very special issues which affect them. Aboriginal people in Canada with disabilities have formed an organization to promote their concerns.

Part Three

Identifying Harassment

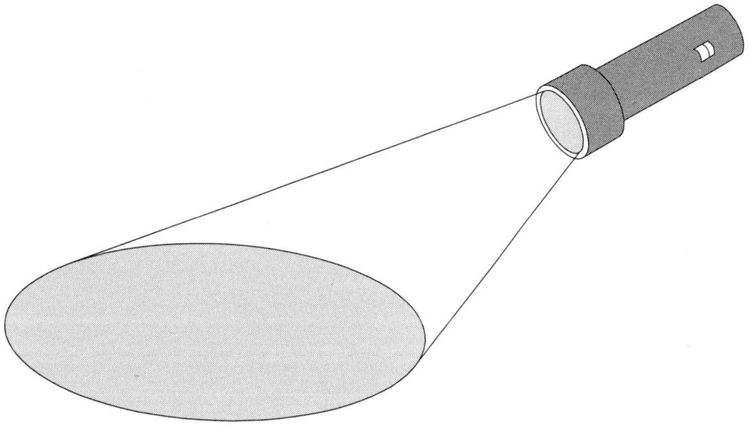

Part Three: Identifying Harassment

Harassment exists in two general forms; overt and subtle. The distinction between the two can be seen from several perspectives. From the point of view of the victims of harassment, overt harassment is easily identifiable while the more subtle may appear to be within the grey area between socially acceptable behaviour and socially unacceptable behaviour.

In both forms, the intention of the perpetrator is of uppermost concern when identifying the actions which may be identified as harassment.

Below, both types of harassment, and some of the concrete forms in which they appear, will be addressed.

A. SUBTLE HARASSMENT

1. Jokes

All cultures and societies contain a penchant for humour. Many studies have been conducted on the sources of humour and the physiological and psychological benefits. There are different types of humour. There are those who enjoy humour with language. There are also those who enjoy what is commonly called 'slapstick' humour.

One of the primary benefits of humour is that it provides stress relief. There is no doubt that humour is beneficial to the workplace, and to productivity, when it reduces stress.

* Some people deal with their fears of the unknown by making jokes.

* The United Nations has commissioned the former president of the Rhinoceros Party of Canada to conduct an international study of humour across cultures.

However, if humour involves increasing stress for any one person, then there is no place for it in the workplace. The creation of a poisoned environment for one person will ultimately lead to a fall in workplace productivity, as stress and tension will increase.

The key issue for many people is identifying what is acceptable humour, and what humour can be classified as harassment. *This issue can be resolved by distinguishing between humour of acceptance and humour of rejection.*

First, in making jokes about a group, the status of the group in the society at large is a key issue. If the group is an established group, the humour may not tend to develop stereotypes of the group, and it is not as likely to adversely affect their political and economic position within society.

* For example, in the nineteenth century, Irish immigrants to Canada were strongly discriminated due to their national origin and because they tended to be Catholics. It has been documented that signs existed in eating establishments at the time which stated "No Irish or Dogs".

  Since that time, the Irish community in Canada has been able to establish its place in Canadian society. In fact, Prime Minister Brian Mulroney is a descendent of those Irish immigrants, and so is former U.S. President Ronald Reagan. Hence, it can be argued that the Irish community in Canada is an established community. Any jokes or humour, reflecting some characteristics of the community, without being demeaning, may be considered an acceptable form of humour.

However, if the group is a vulnerable group, then making jokes about some of the purported characteristics can be damaging and demeaning to the group, and affect the manner in which people may view the group.

* For example, making jokes about women as a group is considered unacceptable, especially jokes related to violence, which predominantly impacts on women, such as rape. **To joke or make statements about a woman being raped, is to implicitly condone that activity or similar activity.**

* Subtly, jokes about "dumb blondes" is an implicit put-down of women with blonde hair. Many women with blonde hair have been stereotyped as lacking intelligence, and only wanting to "have fun". Dumb blonde jokes perpetuate these stereotypes and are a subtle form of harassment of women.

* Making jokes regarding the Sikh community is also considered unacceptable. The Sikh community has been close to the forefront of many cultural issues in Canada, such as the R.C.M.P. allowing turbans as part of its uniform, and some branches of the Royal Canadian Legion insisting that turbans be removed in the halls.

* Jokes about homosexuals are considered unacceptable. The gay community in North America has experienced intense discrimination with outright violent attacks against members of their community in which some have died.

Hence, the first rule to follow with humour is that jokes must be examined as to whether the subject community is vulnerable or established.

Another item to consider when examining jokes about groups, is the objective of the particular joke. Many jokes are made to create a sense of appreciation about characteristics of those groups while others are designed to demean or ridicule the characteristics of that group.

The question to ask is whether the joke looks at the community in a positive aspect, or looks at the community in a negative aspect.

* A joke about a person with a disability which focuses on that disability would be considered unacceptable, but, a joke which disregarded the disability, and perhaps focussed on the abilities or positive characteristics of the person may be considered acceptable.

One manner of applying this rule would be to consider how a member of the group in the joke would react upon hearing the joke. If you feel that a person could be offended, then it is likely that the joke is unacceptable.

Hence, the second rule to follow in humour about groups is to consider whether the humour is a joke of acceptance or rejection. *The joke can be checked by considering whether a person of the group, upon hearing the joke, would be offended.*

There are tactful ways of asking a member of a community or group how they feel about a particular joke prior to using it. Generally, if one expresses sincerity, and the member of the community recognizes the sincerity and sensitivity of the question, then jokes can be checked as to whether they are offensive. However, **it is recommended that where there is doubt about the offensive nature of a joke, it is best to not use it** as different people may have different perceptions about the joke.

The third factor to consider in the telling of jokes is whether the joke promotes prejudices or reinforces stereotypes about a group. There are a number of different types of prejudice which can be built into stereotypes of particular groups. These have all been discussed above in Part II, Section A and Section B.

What tends to be common about all those types of prejudice and their related discrimination is that they involve characteristics over which people may not exercise a great deal of control. These characteristics are determined to some degree by forces of nature; such as natural phenomena (i.e., determination of gender) or a combination of natural phenomena and environmental factors in the upbringing. These characteristics are not necessarily chosen. They are factors over which individuals do not tend to exercise complete control.

Hence, prior to making jokes, the third rule to follow is whether the joke promotes prejudices and reinforces stereotypes in any way. *A manner of checking this rule is to examine the degree to which individuals have control of the particular characteristics which are being highlighted in the joke.*

The above three rules, separately, are necessary conditions for ensuring that jokes not be considered harassment. But separately they are not sufficient. It is only when all three of the above conditions have been met that a joke may be considered to be culturally appropriate.

2. Photographs, Drawings and Written Material

Many people enjoy decorating their work space with various photographs, paintings, drawings and written material that would enhance their office space and differentiate it from other work spaces. The variety and types of drawings always adds to the office, and offers some indication about the type of person in that office space.

Some individuals do not consider the impact of their office decorations on other people. There are those who will display photographs which depict certain groups, such as women, in demeaning photographs or drawings. In other situations, some individuals may display statements or comics ridiculing other people.

The procedure by which to assess the acceptability of photographs, drawings and written material is by the same three rules described above for jokes.

- **1.** Is the subject group or community a vulnerable or established group?

- **2.** Is the concept embodied in the photograph, drawing or written material one of acceptance or rejection of a particular group.

- **3.** Does the photograph, drawing or written material promote stereotypes and reinforce prejudices?

Again, the above three rules are each necessary conditions, but they are not sufficient separately.

3. Qualifications and Meetings

Many minority peoples, including women, notice that they receive differential treatment by others at certain times. This treatment becomes most evident when one first starts a position, and when one is in meetings.

The Questioning

When a minority person starts a new position with an organization, and many of the existing employees have not known the individual previously, the minority person may be asked the question,

"So how did you get this job?"

Upon first hearing, this may appear to be an innocent question. It may be thought that the person asking the question may simply wish to be friendly and start conversation. The person may also be looking to get tips on how to achieve such a position.

There are many innocent reasons why that question will be asked, but there is also a reason related to prejudice why that question is asked.

* The person asking the question may not believe that minority people, including women, have the capabilities and qualifications to do the job. The question is asked to discover whether the person got the job by some means (such as employment equity) other than the merit principle. This is especially true in workplaces where there is an employment equity program, and the employees have not received effective training on understanding the concept and rationale of employment equity.

  Inherently, the questioner holds prejudices, probably because of insecurities about identity and capabilities. He/she is looking for a reason, other than merit, why a minority person, who is believed to be inferior, would get the job in question.

When an individual, whether a colleague or a staff person, asks that question, the minority person should be wary of the intentions, and consider strategies for dealing with those intentions.

The question above can be interpreted as harassment if the person who poses the questions becomes overt about her/his intentions. For example, "Oh, I thought you got the job because of some affirmative action program." The prejudice of this statement is revealed by the questioner assuming that minority peoples can only get jobs if employment equity programs are in place.

If the person is subtle about his/her intentions in asking the question, then there is some doubt about the intentions. In some cases, it is advisable to document the asking of the question in case incidents of harassment or prejudice arise from that same individual at a later date. Then the asking of the question can represent an additional item of evidence.

Meetings

There are a number of tactics used in meetings which can be considered harassment. These tactics are sometimes hidden under the guise of striving for the organization's objectives. These can also be considered political tactics, used in organizations where there is intense competition, to increase the stature of some over others.

For some people, meetings are a public forum where they can increase their own stature at the expense of others.

The first of these tactics in meetings involves individuals disregarding the comments and suggestions of a minority participant. Such actions require that the minority person must be forceful about expressing opinions at meetings in order to retain credibility.

The second tactic is a continuation of the first. If the minority person is not forceful in meetings, then some begin to spread rumours that the person is unprepared for meetings, or raise concerns about the person's competence in achieving the organization's objectives. This may lead to ambiguity regarding the minority person's credibility.

Another tactic used, which is more of a political tactic, is to discuss the issues with a person prior to a meeting, and then present the other person's ideas in the meeting as your own. Such an action is considered plagiarism; claiming the ideas of others as your own.

B. OVERT HARASSMENT

Overt harassment is distinguished from subtle harassment as those actions which can be readily identifiable in terms of acceptable and unacceptable behaviour. Generally, **the intentions of the harasser are made quite clear** through behaviour.

While overt harassment may include the forms of subtle harassment, they involve a more clear objective on the part of the harasser. In terms of sexual harassment, the harasser may be looking for sexual favours. In terms of racial harassment, the harasser may be looking to get the subject fired from the job.

Today, it is generally agreed that the various forms of harassment all have one thing in common: they involve an abuse of **POWER**. The term "sexual harassment" is employed to describe that misuse of power in the workplace which has sexual overtones or implications. In its most frequent application the term is applied to the abuse of power and authority by men towards women. Less frequently, it is applied to cases involving similar abuses of power by women over men, or by members of the same sex over one another, with a view to sexual manipulation, exploitation or degradation.

In all these cases **POWER** is the key element, the condition necessary for the existence of "sexual harassment".

Not all harassment, of course, is sexual in motivation or character. As we have seen, almost any factor can provide a basis for harassment within the workplace. Race, religion, sexual orientation, age, social background, ethnicity, disease, physical disability, family or marital status and, even, weight and physical appearance can become a sufficient basis for harassment.

What all these situations, in their immense diversity, have in common is a dynamic between power and powerlessness. The boss, the supervisor, the executive superior often holds immense power over the career of a subordinate. This power, in turn, may be reinforced and magnified by circumstances and conditions exterior to the workplace. The single-parent may have no other source of income and support; the victim or a dependent may be rendered more vulnerable by virtue of extraordinary medical expenses that happen to coincide with their victimization.

Nor, by any means, is the power dynamic involved in such situations always limited to a simple inter-personal affair between two individuals of unequal status within the hierarchy of the workplace. Often harassment occurs between peers. Women are not infrequently sexually harassed by male co-workers of equal status within the power structure of the organization. Black or other visible minority workers often find themselves in hostile or poisoned work environments where they are pitted against co-workers and cruelly harassed.

In these latter situations, no less than in the former, the key element remains power.

* The power of the co-worker or workers is the power of the group, the power of the collectivity over the individual, rather than the hierarchical power of the superior over the subordinate.

It is, nonetheless, power. In many ways, the abuse of power by a group of peers can be more psychologically devastating and painful than abuse at the hands of a single, more powerful individual. It can also be equally devastating for the victim's career.

In Canada the drift of legal opinion has been decidedly toward the definition of harassment in terms of power. The recent (1991) Ontario case of *Carol Shaw and Levac Supply Limited* is a case in point. Carol Shaw alleged that she had been harassed by a co-worker for fourteen years. Her co-worker, constantly directed derogatory and belittling remarks at her. He mimicked her, made insulting remarks and whistled tunes such as "Slow down, you move too fast" to imply that she was incompetent and slow in the performance of her duties.

While there was no evidence of sexual solicitation and advances or any evidence of an economic threat in the co-worker's behaviour, the Board of Inquiry found that Ms. Shaw had been the victim of sexual harassment as defined in section 6 (2) of the *Ontario Human Rights Code*.

The Carol Shaw case clearly extends the meaning of sexual harassment to include comments that do not, in themselves, constitute sexual advances, threats or solicitations.

In the United States, many decisions have pointed in a similar direction although contrary trends have surfaced in certain jurisdictions. An increasing number of complaints involving men as victims have been primarily responsible for the pressure towards definition in terms of power and the abuse of power. Currently, 10% of all sexual harassment complaints filed with the Equal Opportunities Commission involve men as victims. As the number of women in positions of authority increases, and as the stigmas attached to homosexuality continue, it is expected that such figures will increase and force a serious revision of the concept of harassment within the American workplace.

1. Three Rules for Identifying Harassment

There are a number of different tactics which may be used by individuals when they are harassing overtly. In many instances, these tactics may be overt to the victim, but they may be somewhat subtle to others.

There are three guidelines to follow when identifying harassment.

1. Is behaviour based on a prejudice or a stereotype? *What are the intentions of the harasser in behaving in that manner?*

Examine Part Two of this manual for the different types of prejudice and discrimination which has been considered illegal by provincial and federal human rights codes. The Appendix contains outlines of both federal and provincial legislation for reference purposes.

The organization's harassment policies should be examined in this area. If such policies do not exist, then it may be suggested to the responsible people that these policies be instituted.

2. Is the behaviour unwelcome by the recipient?

Is it behaviour with which the recipient is not comfortable? Would the recipient prefer that the behaviour did not occur, or is it tolerated in order to maintain friendly office relations?

The recipient must also examine his/her own feelings in this area. In many instances, the recipient may ask her/himself whether he/she encouraged this behaviour.

Did I do something to deserve this?

Am I responsible for it?

Did I encourage it?

It is more important for the recipients to assess the behaviour of suspected harassers and their feelings about that behaviour, not their reactions. **Often, people's reactions in stressful situations may not accurately reflect their feelings about that situation.**

3. Is the behaviour continuous? Has it occurred on several occasions, even when warnings have been issued?

An action may be considered harassment if it is continuous over a period of time. If the recipient had warned the harasser that the behaviour is unwelcome, and the behaviour continues, than the behaviour can be considered to be harassment.

The above three guidelines can assist to determine whether particular behaviour is considered to be harassment.

C. SUMMARY OF GUIDELINES FOR IDENTIFYING HARASSMENT

GUIDELINES

FOR ASSESSING JOKES, PHOTOGRAPHS, DRAWINGS AND WRITTEN MATERIAL

1. Is the subject group or community an established community or a vulnerable community?

2. Is the implied objective one of acceptance or one of rejection of the subject group or community?

3. Is prejudice promoted, or stereotypes reinforced, of the subject group or community in any way?

GUIDELINES

FOR IDENTIFYING WHETHER BEHAVIOUR MAY BE CONSIDERED HARASSMENT

1. Is the behaviour based on a prejudice?

2. Is the behaviour unwelcome by the recipient?

3. Is the behaviour continuous over a period of time?

Part Four

How People Respond to Harassment

Part Four: How People Respond to Harassment

INTRODUCTION

North American society has long discouraged the displaying of emotion in the workplace. Our society has placed a great deal of emphasis on the importance of controlling one's emotions in stressful situations in the workplace.

He is grace under pressure. He never sweats. He can handle it.

One of the systemic barriers to, first, women and, second, to cultures where the emotional response is accepted and encouraged, is the North American belief that to display one's emotions indicates a loss of control. As soon as one expresses one's emotions, there is the perception that one is weak and not able to "handle the pressure". Women have been stereotyped as being 'emotional' in a sense that assumes that expressing emotions is negative. Some women are not 'emotional' and there are men who are 'emotional'. These people are viewed almost as mutants in our society:

- She is a real butch. What kind of lady is she? She has no feelings whatsoever.

- He is a wimp, a crybaby. He hasn't got what it takes to get the job done. He can't handle the situation.

As a result of these implicit pressures to behave according to one's gender, some people have been required to hide their true selves behind a mask that is considered more gender appropriate. These individuals are bottling their feelings and hiding themselves. They are being prevented from being themselves. In some sense, they are bottling their emotions.

Recently, psychologists and psychotherapists have debated the value of "bottling one's emotions". Some have argued that the bottle must remain uncapped to discourage the buildup of problems and an increase in stress. Arguments have abounded that to bottle emotions is to merely delay the day when the pressure will break the bottle.

Some counter arguments assert that bottling emotions is unproductive. What some of these people argue is that the emotions should not be bottled, but neither should they be indiscriminately released so that there is an outpouring of feelings. Such a situation, it is contended, can perpetuate the feeling of a loss of control over one's life.

When individuals experience harassment, they likely undergo a series of initial emotional responses to the harassment. Due to the nature of harassment as an expression of power, many people immediately begin to question themselves and their actions.

A. INITIAL EMOTIONAL RESPONSES

Harassment involves a range of psychologically and/or physically violent forms of behaviour. **The victim often suffers profoundly. There are strong similarities between the manner in which victims respond to sexual assault and the manner in which they respond to harassment.**

1. Shock and disbelief

Initially, a person subjected to harassment may experience a feeling of shock, be very surprised and somewhat disoriented by the event. The victim may not have an opportunity to respond to the incident. Some recipients will find themselves responding without realizing it. Others will be prevented from reacting by their surprise.

Most people possess an inherent desire for positive congenial relations with people. Some may not have experienced the negative realities of society as yet. When they do experience these realities, they can be surprised by the unexpectedness of the experience.

2. Anger

The victim may later experience anger toward the perpetrator of the harassment. The anger may stem in part from a feeling that the victim's rights have been violated, and in part, from a sense that the harasser has exercised power unjustly in gratifying his/her feelings.

The victim may experience a strong impulse to lash out at the perpetrator, to force him/her to undergo the same kinds of experiences the victim has felt.

3 A Feeling of Powerlessness

The victim of harassment within the workplace often has much in common with the victim of physical and/or sexual abuse in the home situation.

Harassment is essentially an abuse of power.

The victim, whatever his/her identity, is *relatively* powerless in comparison to the perpetrator or perpetrators. Power has played a very important role in the traditional workplace. For a long time, it was believed that power was held primarily at the top of the workplace hierarchical structure, and it has been primarily held by men. Women have traditionally held subordinate positions in the traditional workplace, and as such have often been subject to the power of men. In many cases, much more often than has been reported, more than a few men have abused their positions of power to sexually harass women. The hierarchical structure of the traditional workplace has contributed to the degree to which harassment has, and is, occurring.

A woman or small group of women in a predominantly male work environment may have to deal with a situation in which they are pitted against a formidable collectivity of fellow co-workers. The entire atmosphere of the workplace may be hostile and poisoned against women. Sexist jokes, nude pin-ups, and sexually explicit conversation may be an accepted and everyday aspect of the environment. In such situations it is understandable that a feeling of powerlessness may be the first response of the victim. The formidable task of altering such setting may seem hopeless.

* Carol Shaw tolerated personal abuse for some fourteen years before she finally felt compelled to quit at a considerable financial and career loss to herself.

The degree of powerlessness experienced tends to be proportional to the severity and duration of the abuse. The sooner the victim realizes the extent of his/her own power and decides to do something about the situation, the better generally for all concerned.

4. Loss of Self-Respect & Dignity

Harassment quickly tends to undermine its victim psychologically. Initially, the situation may be such a radical departure from the ordinary and normal course of life that the victim feels lost and helpless. Few people are prepared and psychologically equipped to deal with such unusual and threatening situations.

In certain cases, this initial loss of social bearings on the part of the victim can lead to a feeling of complicity. The first sexual advances of a superior, for example, may be accepted in numbness, out of simple shock.

For the victim, all harassment situations are intrinsically demeaning. The illegitimate exercise of power by another or others reduces the victim in her or his own eyes to a status that is something less than fully human. The victim feels the loss of the autonomy and freedom which is fundamental to a person's basic dignity and self-respect.

As in other cases of physical and/or sexual abuse the victim often responds with self-blame. What have I done to elicit this reaction from my boss or co-workers? Many victims internalize their abuse in the form of feeling responsible for it. The strong social tendency toward "blaming the victim" is often found to be internalized by the victims themselves. Like those around them, they react by blaming themselves for what they are suffering and enduring.

The loss of self-respect and dignity can result in inaction on the part of the victim to recognize and deal with the harassment. The victim may feel embarrassed or humiliated for being the target of harassment. The victim may fear being ridiculed, or made to feel guilty that they somehow are responsible for the behaviour of the harasser. In many cases, they do not want their spouses, significant others, parents and children to know about their predicament. The overwhelming number of victims of harassment do not action because they fear that a direct confrontation with the harasser would result in threats to their livelihood.

5. Depression

Like all abusive situations, harassment is inescapably depressing for its victims. The extent, depth and seriousness of the consequent depression is, again, a function of the severity and duration of the abuse experienced.

Nervous collapse or breakdown due to harassment in the workplace is not unknown and some have even been driven to the ultimate end of the continuum: suicide.

* In one recent California case, the courts decided that a black man had been physically harmed by the verbal abuse and discriminatory actions of his white co-workers and supervisors. Doctors testified that his diabetic condition had been worsened by the depression and stress he suffered in his place of employment, triggering a general collapse in his health.

Stress is today recognized as a major contributor to many serious health conditions. The stress that is inherent in harassment can result in many physical ailments that can no longer be dismissed as accidental concomitants of such situations.

B. THE VICTIM MENTALITY

There is the danger that **HARASSMENT WHICH PERSISTS UNCHECKED OVER A NUMBER OF YEARS CAN HAVE A PROFOUND EFFECT ON THE RECIPIENT**. Where harassment occurs daily over a period of years, there are few individuals who are strong enough to withstand constant pressure on their personalities.

The victims of harassment can experience a decrease in their self-esteem and self-respect. **The constant battering of their personalities can eventually lead them to believe that they deserve the treatment they are receiving from the harassers.**

Unfortunately, recipients of harassment may reach a stage where they feel isolated and incapable of taking action to stop the abuse. The feelings may further degenerate into a belief that they are undeserving of any support.

The victim mentality can be avoided by recipients of harassment responding quickly and effectively to end the harassment.

C. BEHAVIOUR AS A RESULT OF THE EMOTIONAL RESPONSES

1. Absenteeism & Loss of Productivity

Absenteeism is a less drastic but no less emotional response to harassment. Not unexpectedly, a sharp rise in an employee's rate of absence from work often accompanies and is symptomatic of abuse within the workplace. The victim simply cannot face the harasser or harassers and simply chooses to stay away from work in order to avoid the situation.

Closely related is another symptomatic response: a marked decline in productivity. Workers who are experiencing harassment, naturally enough, find it difficult to cope with their duties.

* Their work time tends to become increasingly absorbed in tormented reflection.

* Their attention is constantly distracted by the presence of the harasser or the threat of further intimidation.

2. Quitting

Many victims of harassment in the workplace simply quit in order to escape from a situation that is unpleasant or unbearable.

* After fourteen years of abuse which her employer failed to stop, Carol Shaw was driven to choose this option.

Apart from the emotional and psychological consequences there are also often serious financial consequences for the victim. Pension plans can be seriously disrupted and, not infrequently, the victim fails to find another or an equivalent position to the one lost.

The sense of injustice experienced by a victim driven to such a desperate expedient is something that may well mark and seriously damage a life.

D. RATIONAL RESPONSES

Many victims, after they have experienced harassment, ask themselves the question, "What could I have done to prevent this from happening to me". They re-examine their own responses and attempt to determine if there was a way in which they could have responded differently and better.

The answer to the question almost always tends to be affirmative when we are dealing with difficult situations. Victims of harassment will find numerous instances where they "said the wrong thing" or didn't say enough when they should have. While these situations are unavoidable, and are natural, they can be developed into a process which will prepare anyone for dealing with a harassment situation.

Below are a number of principles which have been found to be consistent in instances where there has been a rational response to harassment.

1 Learn the emotional responses to surprising and stressful situations.

By understanding the range of feelings which can be experienced in stressful situations, potential recipients of harassment can prepare themselves for recognizing those feelings and using them to their advantage when experiencing harassment. It is important to note that victims must not, and most cases cannot, avoid experiencing these feelings. Generally the first time harassment occurs it is a surprise to the recipient. When individuals are surprised, their emotions tend to govern their modes of response to a situation.

2 Learn the behaviour that is associated with each emotional response.

When individuals learn the particular behaviour that is associated with the emotional responses, then they are more prepared to allow themselves to experience their feelings without having them "run away from them". While it is very difficult 'to keep a cool head' about things during stressful times, having this knowledge can help people to understand themselves better, and develop effective means of dealing with the situation.

3 Objectively examine the behaviour of the harasser.

When people experience harassment, there may be ambiguity with regards to assessing the behaviour of the harasser. Many may ask themselves, "Is this harassment or am I just overreacting?"

When experiencing their emotions, some individuals may be looking at their own behaviour too much, and not looking at the behaviour of the harasser.

Hence, using objective criteria, such as this guide, the victim of harassment can assess whether the actions of the perpetrator constitute harassment and then if necessary take action to end the behaviour.

4 Examine the motivations for the harasser's behaviour.

The harasser always has a motivation for committing harassment. Some of these motivations have been discussed in Section Three, where the reasons for prejudice and discrimination have been outlined. However, generally, the prime motivation for harassment is an exercise of power.

By examining why the perpetrator is doing what he/she is doing, and what the motivations are for needing to exercise power, the victim of harassment can develop a more effective means of halting the activity.

It also helps the victim of harassment to realize that she/he is not at all to blame for the behaviour. Many harassers attempt to lay the onus of responsibility and decision on the victim, implying that any decisions the victim makes in connection with the harassment are her/his own responsibility.

- "Those are your options. Either you meet me at the hotel tonight, or I'll be forced to consider someone else, who would be a better team player, for that special project. Remember, IT'S YOUR CHOICE."

E. EMOTIONAL VS. RATIONAL RESPONSES

As we have noted, reason and emotion are not simple contraries. Harassment is intrinsically and inescapably an emotional experience for the victim. The effective dimensions of the event cannot and certainly should not be denied. They must be dealt with in as sensitive and as effective a way as possible.

In such situations the role of reason is not to deny or repress the emotional aspects of the experience. The role of reason is:

(a) to restrain the emotions from leading us into actions that we will later regret as useless and/or as self-damaging and

(b) to place our experience in a perspective from which possible solutions and escape routes are made visible. Through reasoned response we can at least attempt to mould the circumstances of our lives to our own benefit.

In harassment situations, however, our emotions tend to predominate. **The ability to sit down under such circumstances and think about one's situation and the best and most reasonable courses of action is not an art that comes naturally or easily to many of us.** The control of the passionate emotions that can be roused within an individual by such aggressive behaviour is never an easy matter.

Help and support of others is perhaps indispensable in such states. Professional counsellors can be especially effective and helpful under such conditions. Victims of harassment are often unconscious of the damage done to them emotionally and psychologically. Such damage might be repaired by a sensitive and supportive professional counsellor. On the other hand, if it is not addressed, victims may be rendered incapable of taking a rational approach to their situation.

In most cases, where jobs, and indeed entire careers, are at stake, the cost of private counselling can be a solid investment.

Sadly, it is a fact of organizational life in North America that the institutional process for dealing with complaints about harassment can add to the abuse. During investigations, in tribunal and court hearings, victims of harassment may well find themselves attacked.

* As the Anita Hill/Clarence Thomas hearings before the U.S. senate recently demonstrated, the motives, the honesty, the honor and the very sanity of the complainant may be brought into question.

Victims who press harassment charges are often grilled about their lives and their pasts much as rape victims.

The attempt of the victim to deal with her/his situation rationally may not meet with an equally rational response from the organization and its hierarchy. This makes the matter of external and professional support for the victim of even more imperative consequence. For most of us, it is virtually impossible to maintain a rational stance and perspective when we are surrounded by others acting on the basis of unreasoning emotion.

F. CULTURE & HARASSMENT

1. Gender Differences

A fact has to be faced: harassment is so pervasive a phenomenon within the North American workplace that it is a part of the culture of the continent.

This is, perhaps, especially so for women. Following the Anita Hill/Thomas Clarence affair, extensive surveys and polls were conducted in the United States. The figures that have emerged are startling.

* The *National Association of Female Executives* found that an astonishing 53% of the 1,300 members it surveyed either had been sexually harassed or knew of someone who was.

We forget that the massive movement of women into the North America workplace is a relatively recent and a revolutionary phenomenon within our society. For centuries exclusion and discrimination were the culturally accepted lot of women in western society.

* Women should only be allowed into certain areas of the work force -- the traditionally feminine occupations such as nursing, teaching and social work;
* Women make unsuitable managers, bosses, supervisors and executives;
* Women should be paid less than a man for work of the same nature or of an equivalent value;

These beliefs were all culturally acceptable and unquestioned behaviors a mere three decades ago. That they are today culturally unacceptable is a measure of the social change we have experienced in the course of the past few decades.

Attitudes, however, as deeply rooted in a society as sexism and racism are too fundamental to be eradicated overnight. They are pervasive and unconsciously, as well consciously, influence our behaviour and relations with one another. They are particularly manifest in the unthinking assumptions that we make about each other, often in trivial or seemingly trivial situations.

Below is a view of the similar situations, but with gender bias.

GENDER BIAS COMPARISONS

* A man has a picture of his family on his desk. In some eyes this may make him seem a "solid, responsible family man".	* A woman has a picture of her family on her desk. In some eyes this may be interpreted as a threat to her career or commitment to the company. "Her family comes before her job".
* Two male executives are talking; they must be discussing the latest merger or some other form of business.	* Two female executives are talking; they must be gossiping.
* He's not at his desk, he must be at a meeting.	* She's not at her desk, she must be in the ladies' room.
* He's having lunch with his boss, he's on his way up in the company.	* She's having lunch with her boss! They must be having an affair!
* The boss critiqued his performance; don't worry he'll improve.	* The boss critiqued her performance; she'll be terribly upset.
* He got a raw deal and was treated very unfairly. Did he get angry?	* She got a raw deal and was treated very unfairly. Did she cry?
* He's had another child, he'll need a raise.	* She's having another child, she'll be less committed to the company and will cost us a fortune in maternity benefits.
* He's leaving for a better position. He's smart, ambitious and knows a good opportunity when he sees it.	* She's leaving for a better position. Women aren't reliable. They lack commitment to the organization.

[Based on: "Is This Where I was Going?" by Natasha Josefowitz, (Warner Books, 1983)].

These attitudes are by no means uncommon in the words and behaviours of both men and women within the contemporary North American workplace. They reflect the still deep and pervasive sentiment of sexism that exists within our culture.

In almost all societies men and women are socialized differently. This leads to significant cultural differences between the sexes within given societies. Within many societies the culture of one sex often differs from that of its opposite. Modern industrial society in North America is no different. In spite of the ideal of equality between the sexes and the recent attempt to justly integrate women into the mainstream of the economy, vast, culturally rooted differences in perception still separate the sexes and generate problems. Many aspects of the phenomenon of harassment are rooted in these culturally induced differences in perception of men and women in our society.

Repeatedly, studies in both Canada and the United States have shown that men and women in our culture tend to see sexual harassment -- and indeed harassment in general -- very differently.

Social psychologists have long noted that various forms of harassment-like behaviour are part and parcel of growing up male in North American society. **To a greater or lesser extent men in our society are often socialized to test, tease and/or torment one another.** Such aggressive forms of behaviour between men are, and long have been, accepted and cultivated as part of the masculine ethos of our society. They are believed to raise strong successful men. The dehumanizing aspects of this socialization process have recently been elucidated by such individuals as the American poet, Robert Bly in his book, *Iron John*, and popularized by the new "men's movement" that is sweeping the continent.

Needless to say, such behaviour was, and remains, part and parcel of the traditional, male dominated workplace in our society. Traditionally, men have either learned to deal with such harassment in kind or folded under the pressure of it. Women who do not have the same process of socialization behind them have no intention of doing either. They want fundamental changes in the basic quality of human relations within the workplace and an increasing number of men are prepared to support such changes.

On all levels of our social life harassment is coming into question and social disapproval.

Today, the most common harassment complaint in Canada and the United States involves the charge of a poisoned or hostile work environment. Generally speaking, the racial harassment of minorities is now clearly considered beyond the pale. Few would argue, for instance, that the use of words such as 'nigger', 'chink' or 'gook' are acceptable. And who would condone the display of racially denigratory signs or pictures in offices and locker rooms? By comparison, however, sexism is still socially acceptable.

* Nude pinups of women are still to be found on the walls of trader's cubicles on the floor of the New York Stock Exchange.

* Men in offices across the continent feel free and justified in making denigratory remarks about a woman's pregnancy or imminent menstrual period.

* The term 'bitch' is applied to women far too readily.

Sexism remains a part of the North American male ethos and the values, beliefs, assumptions and actions arising out of that ethos provide the general context in which harassment is understood and dealt with in our society.

The average North American male, for example, is socialized to find sexually explicit language acceptable. **Such talk is "men's talk".** It is part of the ethos of masculinity in our society that such a way of speaking is characteristically male. Men in our society often learn that they are expected to think and speak of women as sexual objects.

Many men, as a consequence, feel their masculinity threatened by female co-workers who take exception to working in environments shaped and dominated by the expression of such attitudes and assumptions.

To some extent, such cultural differences between the sexes can lead to misunderstandings and serious failures of communication. In certain circumstances, women may misunderstand the intentions behind such talk on the part of men. Sexually explicit language may not be intended to intimidate and harass. Men may be, in certain cases, quite unconscious of offending the feelings and sensibilities of female co-workers. Such situations may, however, be quickly and effectively resolved through direct and open confrontation. Once the feelings and concerns of the offended party or parties are known and appreciated, then it can be reasonable to expect the immediate cessation of such behaviour.

2. Cultural Differences

Cultural differences between societies are, of course, often greater than they are between the sexes within a society. Different peoples have different ways of living and behaving, different systems of belief and values that mould and shape the ways in which individuals relate to one another. As a consequence, in certain cases, the behaviour of minority individuals can be misunderstood and misinterpreted as involving harassment.

a. Business and Personal Relations

In many eastern cultures, for instance, business is conducted in settings and circumstances that are more social than is the case in North America. In Canada and the United States people tend to draw a clear distinction between business meetings and social meetings. The latter occur after working hours. 'Socializing' during working hours is frowned upon as frivolous and unproductive in North America.

In the orient, by contrast, the development of personal relations plays a far more significant role in the development of effective business and working relationships. Serious business is conducted only with people one knows and trusts. Therefore, social contact is required to build trust before business can be fully discussed and negotiated.

For South Asians, it is more important that personal relations be maintained than to complete tasks. The reason is that networking plays a very important function in the development of business relationships for South Asians. Knowing a potential business partner in advance has trust already built into the relationship.

This difference is significant and can all too easily lead to misunderstandings and misinterpretations regarding intentions. Social invitations and meetings in the North American business context can easily be perceived as inappropriate and ring warning bells especially in the minds of female executives.

* A Pakistani businessperson may suggest to his/her counterpart that they go for drinks at 2:00 in the afternoon. The counterpart can interpret such an invitation as flirtatious, and may refuse on that basis. The Pakistani businessperson may have been interested only in building a personal relationship for business purposes.

b. Dignity and Saving 'Face'

In many eastern, and in many traditional societies the world over, direct criticism and confrontation is unacceptable. The person subjected to direct criticism "loses face" and can experience acute embarrassment. Such behaviour, in the context of those societies, is perceived as rude, aggressive and intolerable. In mainstream North American life, by comparison, such behaviour is accepted as routine and normal.

* An African Canadian may not tell a person who is harassing him/her that the behaviour is wrong as it would be direct criticism. Instead, he/she is more likely to suffer quietly and live with the problem.

As such, many cultures which value 'face' may use other means to stop the harassment other than directly confronting the perpetrator.

In some instances, confrontation is avoided because there is the possibility that at the conclusion of the confrontation, someone is going to lose face, or dignity. Generally, those cultures which place a strong value on saving face have devised various mechanisms for ensuring that disagreements can be worked out without indicating who has 'lost the argument'.

* A Chinese woman has been invited repeatedly for dinner, despite repeated refusals, by a North American male colleague in a U.S. workplace. The woman refused to confront the man about 'harassment' because confrontation is an unacceptable option for her.

One of the means which is employed to avoid confrontation is the use of a third party. This third party will approach the perpetrator and inform him/her that the behaviour is unacceptable.

Traditional Chinese may deal with problems through the use of third party intervention. The third party may be used as an intermediary or as a mediator.

* A traditional Chinese man was mimicked by co-workers for his Buddhist faith. He had requested leave for a Buddhist holiday at a busy time for the organization. The supervisor had refused on the basis that he could "hum any other time, but not on my time." The man was offended but did not say anything to the supervisor. Instead, he enlisted the aid of a local Chinese politician.

South Asians also prefer to avoid conflict. They may not directly refuse a request, especially in the face of someone who holds more power than themselves. This may give a harasser encouragement to continue if they do not experience outright resistance or refusal.

As in other cultures, there is importance in saving face. Many South Asians may already be experiencing a loss of face due to their educational qualifications not being recognized in North America. This factor, when a South Asian faces harassment, may further compound the problem if the perpetrator is blatantly using power over the individual.

c. Personal Space and Physical Contact

Traditional Chinese may be uncomfortable with members of the opposite sex who give them friendly hugs, taps and other forms of touching. Conversely, members of the same sex may touch without implying a sexual connotation.

On the other hand, Latin American people tend not to be as reserved as mainstream North Americans concerning physically touching other individuals. This can also lead to serious misunderstandings.

In Canada, for instance, people of South American background are often perceived as over-bearing and intimidating simply because they are accustomed to standing closer to persons to whom they are speaking than is customary for Canadians.

* A Latin American woman can give the wrong impression to a mainstream manager by standing too close. The mainstream manager may interpret the closeness as an interest in more than a working relationship while the woman may only be standing at a distance that is comfortable in her culture.

d. Showing Emotions

Latin Americans may also value and be more open in showing emotion and sensitivity in the workplace than mainstream Canadians, particularly when discussion has to do with possibilities and opportunities. Persons of Latin American origin may also use more animated and broader gestures when conversing, or making a point, than would a mainstream Canadian.

Traditional Africans, on the other hand, do not tend to show their feelings. Many will prefer to retain their feelings within them and not indicate that there are problems.

For many Chinese and East Asians, showing one's emotions is indicating that one is unable to control oneself and therefore may be weak. This approach is similar to North American standards for showing emotions, but is more emphasized.

There are a myriad ways in which cultural differences can lead to perceptions of harassment. A sensitivity and awareness of such differences in cross cultural communication styles within the multi-cultural contemporary workplace is the only reasonable hope of avoiding the rise and cultivation of such potentially serious failures in communication.

As a consequence, many minority employees of both sexes, can feel themselves harassed. In the context of their own societies such treatment would almost certainly be construed as deliberate intimidation.

AS A RULE: IF THERE IS SOME BEHAVIOUR WHICH CANNOT BE EXPLAINED, CHANCES ARE THAT THERE MAY BE A CULTURAL EXPLANATION FOR IT.

Part Five

What can be Done about Harassment?

Part Five: What Can Be Done About Harassment?

In the following sections we will examine various strategies from the point of view of (a) the individual, (b) the manager and (c) the organization as a whole for effectively dealing with harassment.

A. STRATEGIES FOR THE INDIVIDUAL

As we saw in the previous unit, a recent American survey revealed that a majority (53%) of female executives questioned had either experienced sexual harassment within the workplace or knew someone else who had. Harassment in all its forms is widespread and prevalent throughout all levels of organizational life in North America.

The individual who directly experiences harassment within an organization must first realize that he/she is not powerless. In Canada such situations are covered by human and civil rights legislation as well as, in some cases, by the criminal code. Internal organization policy must conform with the external requirements of the law and, specifically, of provincial human rights acts and the national Charter of Rights and Freedoms.

Almost all organizations today have a policy for dealing with sexual and other forms of harassment. These policies may be flawed both in formulation and implementation but it is, at least partially, the responsibility of the individual to make such policies work.

Given the great differences in circumstances regarding harassment policies within the Canadian workplace, it is impossible to recommend a universally applicable strategy. There are, however, certain general steps that it is normally reasonable for employees to take in most situations and circumstances. The following steps are offered in a roughly chronological sequence.

Step 1 In most circumstances it is advisable to CONFRONT THE HARASSER(S). Explain how the words and/or actions involved make you feel and make it clear that the behaviour is personally offensive and intolerable. Describe how the behavior is affecting your work and career. Victims ought to be as clear, as definite and as strong as possible in stating their views on such situations.

Much deliberate harassment is the work of cowards and a strong and clear approach often scares them off. Other harassment arises out of sheer ignorance and is conducted under the guise of humour. The confrontational approach can be quickly and effectively educational in such cases.

Step 2 DON'T KEEP THE HARASSMENT SECRET. In many cases the harasser is depending upon secrecy. In others the harasser may expect or require secrecy. Harassers ought to be quickly disappointed in this expectation. **LET CAREFULLY SELECTED, RELIABLE INDIVIDUALS BOTH WITHIN AND OUTSIDE THE WORKPLACE KNOW WHAT HAS OCCURRED.**

Most harassment situations occur in private. It is, therefore, necessary to 'document' the situation. **TELLING OTHERS ABOUT YOUR PLIGHT AND SITUATION AT THE TIME OF ITS OCCURRENCE CAN HELP TO SUBSTANTIATE YOUR CLAIM IF LATER INVESTIGATIONS AND INQUIRIES ARE NEEDED.** In this regard, it is also important for victims to keep any physical evidence of harassment, such as letters or tape recordings.

* When flowers are sent by someone from whom they are not welcome, they should be returned to the florist, indicating that they are not accepted. It is then on record, with the florist, that they were never accepted.

The victim ought, whenever possible, to avoid situations of privacy with the harasser(s). Keep all such dealings as public as possible. This will either deter the offender(s) or provide public confirmation of the situation.

Step 3

SEEK PROFESSIONAL HELP AND/OR COUNSELLING as early as possible. Harassment in the workplace can be as psychologically devastating and harmful as abuse in the home situation. It can be a traumatic experience and it ought to be treated as such. Professional counselling can provide expert and much needed support under the stress of such events.

Recent physiological and psychological studies have repeatedly confirmed the serious implications of stress for general health. Both heart disease and cancer have been linked to stress levels. Harassment increases stress in the workplace. Individuals being harassed ought to do everything within their power to eliminate harassment and reduce stress.

Step 4

INFORM MANAGEMENT OR RELEVANT DEPARTMENTS (I.E. HUMAN RESOURCES OR EMPLOYEE RELATIONS). If the harassment is serious, this ought to be considered as the first step. In certain circumstances it may be inadvisable to confront the perpetrator.

If your organization has a human resource department, or employee relations branch, then it may be useful for the victim to approach them and advise them of the situation. Human resource professionals have training and expertise in dealing with such situations. They may also be able to refer the victim to professional counsellors.

Harassment is not only a personal issue but also a management issue. Such behavior within the workplace can have serious effects on efficiency, productivity and communications. Under these circumstances, it is reasonable to lodge a formal complaint and initiate proceedings against the transgressor under the organization's harassment policy.

If management does not respond, or does not respond adequately to put an end to the harassment, then consider going to higher levels of management, or even outside the organization, to human rights commissions or the courts.

However, a manager, or managers, who fails to deal with a harassment complaint can be implicitly condoning that behaviour, and, therefore, can be liable for harassment charges as well.

Step 5 CO-OPERATE FULLY WITH ANY SUBSEQUENT INVESTIGATION. In too many cases the harasser(s) are let off the hook by victims who, for a variety of reasons, fail to press their cases. Many victims, as mentioned above, feel shame and even guilt over what has happened. Many decide that they "over reacted" and back out of the subsequent investigation. Others may withdraw any complaints due to concerns of job security or concerns of management/peer perception.

Victims must steel themselves for the potential publicity of such an investigation. They must be prepared to have the events in question open to public view. It is, again, in this regard, very important for the victims of harassment to be confident in their own innocence. Often, professional counselling is needed to allow the victims to heal sufficiently to be fully assured they have done nothing wrong and have nothing to be ashamed of.

Sometimes the harasser will claim that the victim is **"trying to ruin my life"**. Such a claim is just a tactic. While it may be argued in the context of justice, **it has often been used to shift the onus of investigation from the harasser to the victim.** Victims and managers who are confronted with harassment cases should not heed such statements.

Step 6 The victim of harassment within the workplace ought to BE FULLY PREPARED TO INITIATE EXTERNAL ACTION through human rights commissions or, if necessary and appropriate, through the courts.

Sadly, in all too many cases, management is either unwilling or unable to effectively stop harassment. In such cases, the victim ought to seek external legal advice. The only rationally effective way of dealing with certain situations, unfortunately, is through the law.

In certain extreme cases such action may, in any event, be advisable. The penalties of organizational policy may not, in the victim's estimation, be severe and appropriate enough for the transgression involved.

B. STRATEGIES FOR THE MANAGER

Managers often feel powerless either to prevent sexual harassment or to deal with it when charges are made. A sense of powerlessness all too often paralyzes action in such situations both on the part of the victim and on the part of those within the organization charged with the responsibility of dealing effectively with such situations.

Consequently, like the victim, the manager must challenge this sense of powerlessness. There are ways of dealing effectively with harassment and, while it may be impossible to eradicate such behavior completely from the workplace, it can be successfully reduced and its consequences mitigated.

In any case, the manager has no alternative but to act. Harassment is perhaps the single most serious problem in the management of human resources within organizations. Apart from the legal and ethical aspects of the issue, harassment is incredibly expensive.

* In a 1988 survey of 160 Fortune 500 companies it was estimated that the phenomenon costs each company an average of 7 million dollars a year. This figure excluded the direct costs of legal defenses against complaints, damages awarded in lawsuits and loss of reputation and business.

Lost productivity, communications problems, unnecessary staff turnovers, absenteeism, external professional aid, compensation and court costs all quickly add up in the costs of inaction.

The following suggestions are designed to assist managers to effectively prepare themselves and their organization for dealing with harassment situations.

1. Effective Preparations for Managers

☑ **KNOW PRECISELY WHAT CONSTITUTES SEXUAL HARASSMENT**. Ensure that all managers within the organization are well informed about the nature of harassment. Much harassment exists simply because the managers responsible don't realize that it is happening. They just don't recognize the phenomenon. They confuse it with humor or playful teasing. They dismiss it as an insignificant matter of personal relations or as a matter of personal idiosyncrasy.

Managers need to be informed about the issues of harassment, and the organization's policies for dealing with it.

☑ **CREDIT THE EXISTENCE OF HARASSMENT.** Many managers know what constitutes harassment but don't believe that it exists within their organizations.

The perfect workplace is a non-existent myth. In reality harassment, in one form or another, exists in every workplace, without exception. The attitude of incredulity on the part of managers confronted with internal charges of harassment strongly acts to discourage the initiation and successful settlement of such cases.

✓ **BE COMPLETELY FAMILIAR WITH YOUR ORGANIZATION'S POLICIES REGARDING HARASSMENT AND ENSURE THAT ALL OTHER KEY MANAGERS ARE ALSO FULLY INFORMED.** Incredibly, in too many cases, charges of harassment are left ineffectively in limbo by managers who are ignorant of their own organization's policies and procedures for dealing with complaints.

✓ **PUBLICIZE THE ORGANIZATION'S POLICY REGARDING SEXUAL HARASSMENT AS WIDELY AND AS FREQUENTLY AS POSSIBLE.** A deliberate and careful educational campaign ought to surround this publication of policy. All employees ought to be made clearly aware of what constitutes harassment and the consequences of indulging in it. All employees ought to have a clear idea of the procedural process by which they can pursue charges against harassers.

Make sure that all managers and employees understand that the workplace extends to lunch breaks and all other social gatherings related to work.

✓ **WHEN COMPLAINTS ARE MADE, HANDLE THEM SENSITIVELY AND PROMPTLY.** Like rape charges, complaints about harassment are not often made lightly. The consequences are too unpredictable and the process of investigation too harrowing for many people to make false accusations and initiate formal proceedings.

Make sure that the organization's formal procedure for dealing with harassment complaints is strictly followed. It is important that complaints are investigated and dealt with as promptly as possible. **Leaving cases on the back burner in the vague hope that they go away is one of the worst possible courses of action.**

✓ **BE SUPPORTIVE OF THE VICTIM.** Realize that such situations involve a great deal of stress and make any allowances and adjustments necessary or desirable under the circumstances.

Be conscious of the fact that the victim may be in need of professional help and counselling. Aid and support the victim in finding such external assistance when necessary or desirable.

✓ **DON'T EXPECT VICTIMS TO KEEP SECRETS.** Many managers resent the fact that victims of harassment feel the need to tell others outside the workplace of their victimization. Encourage victims to find what personal support and encouragement they can, where they can. The reputations of organizations are damaged, ultimately, more by organizational insensitivity than by the actions of individuals within the corporation or institution.

✓ **BE SENSITIVE TO THE RIGHTS OF ALL THE PARTIES INVOLVED IN SUCH ACTIONS.** Harassment complaints often involve charges that are embarrassing to all the parties concerned. Often, the victims are as or more embarrassed and ashamed than the perpetrator(s).

While victims should be fully encouraged to see that they have done nothing wrong and nothing to be ashamed of, discretion and confidentiality are often needed. Investigations ought to be conducted with as much confidentiality as is compatible with a full and complete exploration of the case and its facts. Such investigations cannot be conducted with an assurance of anonymity to either or both parties.

✓ **IF THE WORKPLACE IS UNIONIZED, UNION INVOLVEMENT IN SUCH CASES IS GENERALLY ADVISABLE.** The aim of such policies is to reduce and eradicate harassment from the work environment and this cannot be achieved without the full and harmonious agreement and co-operation of labour and management.

Ensure that the penalties in place for harassment are appropriate. First offenses, if serious enough, may well deserve dismissal.

Make sure that all penalties are paid and that the behavior in question has ceased. Sometimes, perpetrators find different ways of continuing the harassment or of getting back at the victim.

Make concerted and serious periodic attempts to determine the nature and extent of harassment within the workplace. This can be done through such instruments as focused interviews, discussion groups or employee surveys.

Such measures can reveal surprising pictures of what is going on unknown to management within an organizational environment. They can also allow managers an effective way of assessing the effectiveness of the harassment policies and procedures in place.

A common, emotional response to harassment at work is for the victim to quit and seek employment elsewhere. All employees leaving a firm should be carefully interviewed to ensure that they are not leaving due to harassment.

2. Steps for Dealing with a Harassment Case

The following are general steps which managers can follow when an employee confronts them with a harassment case. These are general steps which can be a reference for managers, but they should not take precedence over the organization's procedures.

The steps will begin when a victim approaches the manager with a harassment complaint. It is important that the manager:

A. be as sensitive as possible to the victim's feelings.

B. remain as fair as possible to all parties involved.

Step 1 LISTEN TO THE VICTIM. Note the details of the complaint. Note the victim's name, position, department, etc. and the accused harasser's name, department, etc. You should document all the details of the meeting as they will prove to be useful in an investigation.

Carefully note the victim's complaint. **Ensure that through the discussion, you remain sensitive to the feelings of the victim**. Ask the victim for details of the harassment, i.e. the nature, the time frames, possible witnesses, etc..

Ensure that the victim describes the impact of the harassment on her/his personal heath, and on his/her productivity in the workplace. It is important to gauge the impact of the behaviour on the victim.

* **Remember: Ask open ended questions**. That is, ask questions which do not require a yes/no answer

Step 2 CLARIFY YOUR PERCEPTIONS WITH THE VICTIM. Harassment is a sensitive and difficult issue. You want to ensure that you understand the victim very clearly. Misunderstandings and misconceptions can lead to problems further down the road. Confirming all the details, as you understand them, with the victim will ensure that any possible communication problems can be resolved in advance. This will also ensure that your notes are accurate and complete.

Step 3 EXPLORE THE INFORMAL PROCESS FIRST. Ask the victim if she/he have confronted the accused harasser with the problem. If the victim has not, then that may be the next most logical step. If the victim has, but the behaviour has not changed, then an informal warning from yourself, the manager, may be required to change the behaviour or the formal process may be needed.

Step 4 **CONFRONT THE ACCUSED HARASSER WITH THE COMPLAINT.** Ensure that you have reviewed the notes from your meeting with the victim. Re-examine all the details, and note down your approach before the meeting.

Ask the harasser open-ended questions about his/her relationship with the victim.

If the accused does not acknowledge that any problems have occurred, then go to **Step 5**. If the accused acknowledges that the victim is correct in details, and that the behaviour did not intend the resulting impact on the victim, then there is the possibility that an informal meeting of the victim, the accused and yourself, the manager, may suffice to end the behaviour and facilitate understanding between the victim and the accused. **Such an arrangement is ideal to ensure that the work environment remains friendly and productive.**

If the harasser refuses to acknowledge that the behaviour was unacceptable, then go on to **Step 5**.

Step 5 **INFORM THE ACCUSED HARASSER OF THE NEXT STEPS OF THE PROCESS.** Advise him/her of the organization's sexual harassment policy, and pertinent provincial legislation (i.e. human rights codes). Inform the accused that a formal investigation will take place and describe the process of the formal investigation, the individuals involved in the investigation and the possible actions that will be taken for various outcomes of the investigation. **Assure the accused that you intend to be as fair as possible, but also that if the committee finds that they have harassed the victim, then disciplinary action will take place.** Inform the accused of the range of disciplinary action.

If your organization has not developed a formal harassment investigative process, then it is advisable to begin the development now. See Part V, Section C, § 2, for some key points for a formal process.

3. Strategies for Reconciliation

Strategies for reconciliation generally include conflict resolution processes. When an organization has dealt with a specific problem, it has not necessarily eradicated the problem, but may have merely caused the problem to "go underground" where it may resurface at another time.

Conflict resolution processes provide a means for eradicating the problem. Essentially, an employee who refuses to face the supervisor who disciplined him/her for a harassment complaint has not resolved the conflict. Conflict resolution calls for understanding and commitment and a willingness to listen on the part of both the victim, the supervisor and other parties.

The most common cause of inter-group conflict in the workplace is a simple failure in communication and interpersonal relations.

When communications problems do arise, as they invariably will in any organization, it is generally recognized that the worst course of remedial action is to fix the blame on one person or group of persons.

Depending on the severity of the harassment, and the original intent of the harasser, it may be advisable to inform the harasser that he/she is not 'wrong', but that some actions, but not all, have been deemed to be unproductive for the organization. **Lay the blame on the actions of the harasser rather than on his/her personality.** In other words, allow the harasser to 'save face'.

* When any individual or group is singled out for such condemnation, the result can only be to increase the tensions and probability of future conflict.

* Communication is always a two-way street. It takes two parties for communication to break down. To assign blame to one party is to ignore this basic reality of the situation. It is both a careless and a self-defeating way to deal with a very touchy situation.

Professional help may well be needed by managers to pinpoint the trouble spot or spots in the process and take effective remedial action.

It has been found that one of the most constructive ways of fostering conflict resolution is by employing the inter-group problem solving method. In spite of its name, the method is relatively simple.

* Inter-group problem solving methods often use **a mediator** who is skilled in interpersonal relations and in conflict resolution.

* **The mediator or facilitator sits down with the parties involved. Together they confront the communication problems involved.** Effective procedures are devised to avoid future misunderstandings and conflicts. It has often been found that even when these procedures are afterwards abandoned, communication is improved, conflict and tension lessened.

* The simple process of sitting down together with an impartial and skilled outsider, and openly confronting the problems is often sufficient to heal the wounds of the past.

* The mediator or facilitator needs to be skilled in cross-cultural communications where the conflict involves more than one cultural group.

Managers, leaders, supervisors and mediators at all levels ought to employ and encourage the use of certain simple strategies for improving communication with a view to reducing and resolving conflict and tension within the organizational environment. The following are some examples:

Encourage Expression

When a conflict situation has been identified, all those involved ought to be encouraged to express their feelings and opinions, openly, frankly and honestly. The origins of many tensions and of many open conflicts within an organization lie in the repression of feeling and the suppression of opinion.

Encourage Listening and Paying Attention

One of the chief sources of conflict is the simple fact that the individuals involved are not listening and not paying sufficient attention to one another. Occasionally, this is the case on the part of only one of the parties involved. At other times, it is the situation with both parties or all those involved.

* The role of the leader or mediator in such situations is the delicate one of nurturing and improving the quality and character of attention paid to one another by those involved.

* Individuals involved in these situations ought to be encouraged to ask one another open-ended questions after they have given expression to ideas, feelings or opinions. Employ and request the use of such expressions as:

  "What do you think of...?"

  "How do you feel about...?"

* Where understanding has failed or is uncertain, ask the individuals involved to paraphrase or summarize, in their own words, what has been said. The mediator or leader ought to also paraphrase what has been said in order to demonstrate attention and understanding. Ask such open-ended questions as:

  "You are worried about...?"

  "You think that...?"

Encourage Agreement

Make use of directive questions in order to encourage individuals in conflict situations to talk about matters on which they agree:

"Then you agree that...?"

"You said you wished to...?"

C. STRATEGIES FOR THE ORGANIZATION

If an organization hasn't had any harassment problems as yet, chances are that they will in the near future. Like alcoholics and addicts, organizations that wish to deal effectively with workplace harassment must, first of all, recognize that they have a problem, and that the problem is a serious one. A basic contact with reality is a prerequisite for the formulation and implementation of successful policies in this area of human resource management.

Organizations must realize that harassment exists and that it exists in all corporations and institutions and at all levels.

In the past, **organizational elites have tended to see harassment as a minority problem**. Sexual harassment was a problem for women. Harassment based on race was a problem for visible minorities. It is now, increasingly, being recognized that harassment is a tremendous problem for organizations themselves. Few can afford the financial losses and headaches involved in not successfully dealing with harassment situations.

In a sense, the problem was and remains a minority problem. The problem minority, however, is the minority at the top.

* In North America most corporate and organizational elites are still largely (and in some cases exclusively) composed of white, Anglo-Saxon men. This situation is slowly changing as women and visible minorities begin to break through the infamous "glass ceiling". Nevertheless, the white, Anglo-Saxon male remains the primary source and inspiration in this area of organizational policy in North America.
* In our society, such individuals rarely experience discrimination and harassment. This fact has, in the past, allowed, and continues to allow, many of the key policy and decision makers in the organizational life of the continent to ignore or underplay the significance of harassment.

It is of crucial importance that the managerial elite of a corporation or organization sensitize themselves to the nature and significance of the phenomenon. This constitutes the first step in the development of a successful policy for dealing with harassment on the organizational level.

It is the elite of an organization who set the tone. If that elite tends to underplay the significance of a phenomenon like harassment within the work environment, its attitude and behavior is certain to be diffused downward through the ranks. **Unconsciously and unintentionally it is sending a message that says: harassment will be tolerated.**

Nor are managerial elites immune to the practice of harassment. It is of extreme importance that executives and managers, especially at the highest levels of the organization, act as favorable role models.

All such individuals should be fully conscious that what they say and do on even the most casual occasions is as, or, even more important than formal pronouncements. For such highly placed persons, actions do often speak far louder than mere words.

While developing and producing a comprehensive harassment policy is the first step, it should not be the only step. Organizations need to commit efforts to train managers of the issues of harassment, and to ensure that they understand and support the concept. At the same, orientation programs for new employees, and refresher courses for existing employees should include training on the organization's harassment policy, and the strategies for dealing with situations of harassment.

1. What Must a Successful Harassment Policy Contain?

1. It is, first of all, important to note that all policies for defining and handling harassment charges must be formulated in accordance with existing provincial and federal human rights legislation.

2. Policies should clearly define what constitutes harassment, citing specific examples of prohibited behavior.

3. Policies should include strong and specific penalties for violations. In the worst cases, it should be clear that immediate dismissal will be considered appropriate.

4. Policies should specify definite procedures for victims to follow in the making of complaints. These procedures must contain clear and

definite provisions for circumventing supervisors and organizational superiors who are accused of guilt and/or complicity in particular cases.

It is advisable that, wherever possible, organizations appoint individuals to be solely responsible for the handling of such complaints.

Such designated personnel are ideally placed to survey and report on the quality of the working environment within their organizations. They may directly test and evaluate the effectiveness of the harassment policies in place.

5. Where possible, policies should provide alleged victims with an advisor. Ideally, this person ought to be a professionally trained counsellor who can give victims and alleged victims expert advice on procedures, options and means of best handling such situations and their after effects. Such counsellors can also help by referring victims to external sources of professional help where necessary.

6. Policies ought to stress the responsibility of managers to prevent, discourage and effectively deal with such situations. Penalties for failing to do so and/or for obstructing the complaint and investigation process ought to be specified and strongly defined.

In most jurisdictions in Canada persons in positions of authority are held responsible under human rights legislation for preventing or stopping such behavior. They can be held liable along with the perpetrator.

7. Policies should contain provision for periodic publicity and training campaigns on the subject of harassment.

Employees should be reminded periodically that the top levels of management are strongly committed to the policy and dedicated to the eradication of harassment within the workplace.

Training seminars aimed at sensitizing workers to the issue and what is involved should be held at all levels of the organization and on a recurring basis.

8. Successful policies also often contain an alternative procedure to the one governing formal complaints. In some instances the behaviours involved are either borderline or largely unintentional and the victims, while distressed, may not feel comfortable with initiating formal complaints.

A policy which allows for private conflict resolution in such cases, outside of the formal complaint and investigation process, often works well.

9. It is of vital importance in defining and implementing such policies that the top levels of management are just as much subject to their provisions and penalties as the lower levels. Harassment claims against the managerial elite of an organization must be investigated as thoroughly as those against the lower levels of workers. The penalties for those at the top must be at least as severe and probably ought to be even more severe. The more highly placed the offender, the greater the damage an individual can do to the reputation and well-being of an organization.

10. Policies must include follow up provisions. Someone must be responsible for seeing that all penalties are actually enforced and that the situation has been effectively settled to the satisfaction of the victim.

It is of crucial importance to ensure that no retaliation is taken against the victim for pursuing a complaint. This is possible even if the perpetrator is fired. Friends of the ex-employee within the organization have been known to destroy the careers of such individuals. The evaluation and promotional records of victims should be monitored afterwards and such individuals interviewed by those in charge of administering the policy.

11. It is also advisable that the policy contain a mechanism for healing or reconciliation. After a harassment situation, some individuals may be experiencing strong feelings about either the victim, co-workers or managers who had sided against them. It is important for the effective operation of the organization that these animosities be resolved whenever possible. See Part V, Section C, § 3, above.

If the employees of the organization have a union, then it is advisable to get the union involved in the development of a harassment policy. Have the union issue a statement of support for the policy, and get approval for the process of investigation and the range of disciplinary action for harassers.

Union support can be crucial to the success of a harassment policy.

2. Key Points for a Formal Investigative Process

A. Form an investigative committee of, perhaps, three people who are objective and who are knowledgeable about harassment issues and policies.

B. Develop a methodology which ensures fairness to all concerned, which considers the feelings and sensitivities of all concerned, which is **confidential and which is fair and just**. Usually, interviews with all witnesses, with other employees who may have experienced harassment from the same accused, and with co-workers of both parties are part of the methodology. Some organizations have tended to bring in outside experienced consultants to carry out the investigative approach. This is ideal from the standpoint of objectivity and fairness for all concerned.

C. Make special work arrangements, or leave, for the victim and the accused to ensure that they are not in contact during the investigative process.

D. Develop a set of guidelines for action, based on the various possible outcomes of the investigative process. Disciplinary action would be included here.

E. Develop strategies for healing, or reconciliation, after the issue has been dealt with on the formal level. Remember that these people may have to come into contact again through work arrangements. By developing a healing or reconciliation process, both employees may be comfortable with working with each other in the future.

See Part V. Section C. (previous section) for suggested strategies for reconciliation.

If the reconciliation or healing is not successful, then transferring the accused, or the victim if the victim desires, may be necessary.

Ensure that all employees are aware of this process.

Part Six: Case Studies

Part Six: Case Studies

INTRODUCTION

The following case studies are based on actual incidents of harassment that have occurred within Canadian workplaces. **The names, places, settings and dialogue are fictional but the issues are real.**

The cases are offered as illustrations of harassment in its varied forms and to present common dilemmas faced by managers and supervisory personnel in the day to day administration of an harassment policy.

CASE STUDY #1

It is almost ten years, Catherine thought. Ten bloody years since she had started her job as dispatcher for the courier service. They had not been the best working years of her life. From the beginning, she had felt uncomfortable and out of place in the almost exclusively male environment of the shipping and receiving plant.

Daily, there were small, almost petty incidents. Pinpricks that seemed individually insignificant but which had left an accumulative mark that surely wasn't insignificant. Catherine thought about quitting. She was deeply unhappy in her job or, to be more precise, she was deeply unhappy about the work environment of her job. The situation at work was affecting the whole of her life. Involuntarily, on her days and hours off, she found herself thinking about its irritations and feeling the resentments that had gradually built up over the years. The atmosphere of the plant and the office were poisoning, it seemed, the whole of her life.

Could she quit? While the idea was attractive from the point of view of providing an immediate escape, it had serious drawbacks and consequences. The economy was in one of its perennial slumps and the unemployment figures were hardly encouraging. As a single mother with a twelve-year-old son to support, she simply could not face long term unemployment. Besides, she thought angrily, I've invested ten years of my life in the service of this company and if I start over elsewhere I lose everything, seniority, pension contributions, medical and dental plans.

She stared into her coffee cup. What could she do? She had never felt more alone or so trapped. A few days ago, she had thumbed through an employee brochure on the subject of sexual harassment and contemplated launching a complaint.

The thought of doing so was almost as threatening and daunting a prospect as the thought of quitting and attempting to find another job in a time of severe economic recession. It all seemed hopeless. She knew full well the uproar such a complaint would produce. And for what, she wondered. Do I really have a case? Her situation largely seemed a complication of petty annoyances and minor grievances that could all too easily be dismissed as unworthy of consideration under the company's policy on sexual harassment within the workplace.

According to the brochure, the first steps in the policy advocated an attempt at informal settlement. Confront the offending parties, the pamphlet had advised. Catherine smiled bitterly to herself. She had gained various unflattering nicknames within the plant for having done just that. The "feminist" and, more frequently, the "feminist bitch" were, she knew, favourite ways of referring to her in certain quarters.

Incidents from the past flooded into mind. There had been the infamous Christmas party of a few years past. She had been the only female employee present. The other women had been the wives or dates of her fellow employees in the plant. At one point in the festivities, Hank and several of his cronies from the sorting plant had produced one of those life-size inflatable dolls that are sold in seedy men's magazines. As a supposed 'joke', he and several of the others had caressed and made obscene actions and gestures toward the thing.

Catherine had been outraged. Their performance struck her as not only unspeakably vulgar but as degrading and contemptuous of women in general. It seemed to her that their actions not only ridiculed women but made fun of rape. She had been furious and she had made a scene.

She had let the men involved know exactly what she thought of their little act. In response, they had merely laughed and made certain snide and drunken insinuations about her sex life. Several of the other women present had surrounded her in an attempt to calm her down and defuse the situation. They obviously thought it was a matter of no great importance. Just the usual case of "the boys" being crude, vulgar and drunk. She had failed to find any support from the other women present and several had made her feel as if she were being pretentious and acting inappropriately in the context of the annual Christmas staff party.

Only a few days ago, she recalled, she had confronted the men in the sorting room over a calendar they had hung in the office area. It depicted various naked 'playmates' for each month of the year. They had only laughed and, in effect, told her to mind her own business. "If it offends you, don't look", had been the response of Sam, the supervisor of the sorting facility.

Catherine's work life in the plant had been a continuous history of such incidents. She had spoken out often and had always insisted on letting the perpetrators know that their actions were offensive and unwelcome in her presence.

Case Study #1 Exercises

1. Was Catherine right to respond as she did over the 'doll' and calendar incidents? Why or why not?

____

____

____

____

2. Do such incidents constitute harassment of a sexual character? Why or why not?

____

____

____

____

3. If the other women at the infamous Christmas party were not particularly offended or upset by the behavior of Hank and his buddies, did Catherine have the right to react and respond as she did?

____

____

____

____

4. Since Catherine is, obviously, the only person unhappy with her work situation, should she quit or learn to live with its realities? Is it fair in such situations for one person to demand that everyone else change to accommodate him/her?

____

____

____

____

Case Study #1 Discussion Notes

1. Was Catherine right to respond as she did over the 'doll' and calendar incidents? Why or why not?

   Catherine had to respond to the doll incident the way she did because the manner in which "the boys" were having fun was similar to the "jokes" and needling at work. They were challenging her gender and attempting to "put her down". It is very important that Catherine not tolerate this behaviour and indicate to the men how she felt.

2. Do such incidents constitute harassment of a sexual character? Why or why not?

   Yes they do. The doll incident and the calendar are indicative of women being treated like objects. The men were plainly focussing on Catherine's gender rather than her capabilities.

   The doll incident showed that the men were insensitive to the issues facing women, especially when they "joked" about such things as rape.

3. If the other women at the infamous Christmas party were not particularly offended or upset by the behaviour of Hank and his buddies, did Catherine have the right to react and respond as she did?

   Yes. It is irrelevant as to whether others are offended or not. Catherine was offended, and it is important that Catherine have the right to express her beliefs as such. It is important to note here that while the issue is one of sexual harassment, it is not necessary for the offended party to be a member of the offended group. For example, in South Africa, while the issue is one of racial discrimination, there are still some white people who have fought against Apartheid while there have been blacks who have collaborated with the Apartheid government.

4. Since Catherine is, obviously, the only person unhappy with her work situation, should she quit or learn to live with its realities? Is it fair in such situations for one person to demand that everyone else change to accommodate him/her?

   First, Catherine should neither quit nor accept the situation. She should change the environment at her workplace.

   One of the principles upon which our society guarantees our freedom is that we are free to do anything until it impinges on the freedom of others. If one person's rights are being denied for the sake of others, then the above principle has been violated and freedom for all of us is in jeopardy.

CASE STUDY #2

At first Stacy was merely disappointed and depressed. She had just emerged from a meeting with the promotions committee and had learned that she would not be promoted to a management position with the company. She leaned back in her office and recounted the details of the meeting.

Ernest Shipka, Director of her division and the chair of the Committee had begun positively. However, his words of praise and commendation for her work at the beginning of the interview now rang hollow.

He had spoken for the committee and delivered its considered judgment on her application for the management position. The rest of the committee had sat on watching and listening.

"Stacy, in spite of your excellent work with the company, we cannot at this time recommend you for a management position. There have been instances in the past where you have used up all your sick time and have taken additional time-off which indicates to us that you will not have the flexibility nor the commitment required for a management position."

Stacy had been shocked and surprised by this judgment.

"But, Mr. Shipka, you know that I was taking sick days because my son was ill. And when I took leave...."

"Yes, yes. I don't want to argue with you. In fact, I am even surprised that you are arguing. You should be grateful that we haven't fired you."

Stacy was speechless.

"Besides, even if we were to promote you, then our sick policy and our leave policy will be undermined. We would be telling all other employees of the company that commitment to the company and attendance on the job are not important when it comes to promotions. I'm afraid that we cannot give you this position."

He had gone on to note that management had refrained from assigning her the most complicated and demanding projects as a result of her need for time-off to care for her sick child. They were also considering her limited time schedule and inability to take long and lengthy field trips out of town. He went on to say that it was the general opinion of the committee members that the work she did was excellent but that she would not be appropriate for a management position. He concluded that they all felt that her candidacy could not be considered again unless she was able to demonstrate a commitment to the company and regular attendance to the office. He then showed her to the door.

Stacy had, at first, been too shocked and surprised by this judgment to respond. Desperately, she scoured her work history to determine if her performance had at any time been lacking. She knew that management positions did not indicate that the amount of sick leave taken would be a consideration for the positions.

Stacy realized that her son's illness had forced her to take time-off quite regularly from the office, but she always took work home with her and got it done on time and properly. Whenever she had to leave the office to take her son to the doctor she had called in to ensure that everything was all right.

She also recalled that none of the senior management had ever asked her to do special projects or even approached her to take projects involving travel. She felt angry that the opportunity was never raised before, and that she had never been given the opportunity to decide for herself. She knew that she might have taken those projects, and that her mother wouldn't have minded taking care of Justin on occasion.

Now, here they were telling her that in spite of the quality of her performance, she would not be considered for the promotion to management! She knew that requirements for management positions did not indicate that applicants must have a good sick leave record.

At that moment, the phone rang, interrupting her thoughts. She felt frustrated, and was tempted not to answer the phone. But she did anyway.

"Hello."

"Hi Stacy, its Cynthia. Can I talk to you for a moment?"

Cynthia Sandori was the only woman on the Promotions committee. In fact, she was the only woman in senior management in the company.

"Sure, what is it?"

"I want to talk to you about the meting this morning. I want to tell you that there is no one on the committee who disputes the quality of your performance, including Ernest Shipka. You have drawn clients to the firm and your work has been consistently praiseworthy. What is at issue here is not the quality of your work. Rather, it is simply your commitment to the company. Your skills and achievements are outstanding and there is no question that your promotion would be forthcoming, if you weren't away so much."

Stacy listened, but with a growing feeling of resentment and injustice as Ms.Sandori continued. "As a senior member of management, I worked a minimum of seventy hours a week", she continued, "and so did the rest." These long hours, she noted, were not simply evidence of dedication, for they had also served to give her and her colleagues an invaluable feel for the company's "distinctive culture" and an almost intuitive "understanding of its needs".

"If we were to promote you", she concluded, "without demanding an equal commitment to the firm, we would be setting a dangerous precedent that could well wreck the successful and long-standing basis of this company. We would be telling our employees that we no longer value dedication, commitment and career motivation. And, we would be breeding a new stock of employees who neither understood the company sufficiently to respond to its ever changing needs nor shared in the old culture that had shaped its success in the past."

It was an eloquent and obviously sincere speech. Ms. Sandori was a woman of clear and forceful opinions. It was, however, a speech that was far from satisfying from Stacy's perspective. She decided that she really had little choice. She looked up the phone number to the human rights commission.

Case Study #2 Exercises

1. Is this a case of harassment or discrimination? Give reasons as to why or why not?

2. What did Ernest Shipka say to indicate that management may have been discriminating?

3. If you were hired as an advocate for Stacy, what counter arguments would you present against those offered above by the members of the promotions committee?

4. Does Stacy's situation mean that she could not be considered on an equal basis with the full-time employees for a promotion?

5. Can you suggest a compromise approach in this situation?

Case Study #2 Discussion Notes

1. Is this a case of harassment or discrimination? Give reasons as to why or why not?

   It should be fairly evident that Stacy's family status is that of a single mother. There had been no mention of her child's father. The one instance where Stacy may have mentioned her child's father, she indicated her mother (when she considered that her mother could care for her son on occasion.)

   Ernest Shipka indicated that Stacy might have been fired. He was evidently threatening her.

2. What did Ernest Shipka say to indicate that management may have been discriminating?

   He had said that management had refrained from asking Stacy to do special projects as a result of her need to take care of her sick son. It is a case where Stacy's family status, as a single mother, caused her to lose job opportunities because management assumed that her commitment was to her child first and foremost.

3. If you were hired as an advocate for Stacy, what counter arguments would you present against those offered above by the members of the promotions committee?

   An advocate might argue that the number of single mothers has increased dramatically in the last few years. To informally require that potential managers should be accumulating sick days may be interpreted as discrimination on the basis of Family Status against many single mothers who may also be very competent managers.

4. Does Stacy's situation mean that she could not be considered on an equal basis with the other employees being considered for promotion?

   From what Ernest Shipka and Cynthia Sandori said to Stacy, they both believed that she would have filled all the requirements for a management position. But, all their arguments for refusing her had to do with her special situation, not with the her capabilities relative to other candidates.

5. Can you suggest a compromise approach in this situation?

Management may want to consider instituting special measures for single parents. They may wish to consider setting up flexible work schedules, or allowing managers to work some of their hours at home. These would allow competent individuals with special family needs to contribute both to their family and their employer.

CASE STUDY #3

Howard was furious. The promotion ought to have been his. After twenty-seven years with the company, and his recent successful completion of a degree in marketing techniques and technologies, he was more than qualified to fill the position. Still, he had been passed over in favour of a younger man with half his experience and no professional qualification in the field.

Ever since Donald Thompkins had become head of the department, Howard had suspected he was in for a difficult struggle. At twenty-nine Thompkins was the youngest Vice-President in the history of the corporation and it was a fact about which he seemed inordinately proud.

Thompkins appointment had, or so it seemed to Howard, marked a change and turning point in the atmosphere of the office. Several older employees had been, he thought, rushed into early retirement. An influx of young people had occurred, as if overnight, and all the recent promotions had gone to employees in their twenties and thirties. Once, Howard had overheard his new boss talking about getting rid of 'dead wood'.

The talk in the staff lounge and in the formal and informal meetings he attended within the department had made Howard increasingly uncomfortable. At fifty-one, he hardly considered himself over the proverbial hill but Thompkins and many of his younger colleagues gave him the distinct impression that he was, at the very least, hovering on the crest.

Since Thompkins arrival, there had been much talk around the office about the need for "vigor", "freshness" and "enthusiasm". On more than one occasion, Howard had felt intimations to the effect that these were qualities he and several of the older men and women on the staff lacked. In one conversation, with an ambitious younger colleague who was working in close co-operation with Thompkins, she had pointedly referred to "experience" as "'the school master of fools'". This quotation, Howard suspected, was a none too subtle reference to a marketing strategy he had recently proposed. His idea had been rather curtly dismissed as "unimaginative" by Thompkins and his "cutting-edge" assistants.

The final straw, however, had been his meeting this morning with Thompkins. When he had learned that he had been passed over for the supervisory position in the marketing section, Howard had made an appointment with his boss to obtain a full explanation of the reasons involved in the decision.

Thompkins had received him cordially. He had been extremely apologetic about Howard's failure to gain the promotion. He had praised his dedication and competence. "To be honest, Howard," he had continued, "you were in many ways the better candidate for the position. There is no denying that you have more experience than Johnson and you do have a degree in the area. However, experience is really not what the position requires. We were looking for someone capable of breaking with the patterns of the past. We decided, after much and serious consideration, that experience in this context might well hinder the process. Given the current state of the economy and the cut-throat competition we are currently facing, we decided that we have no choice but to opt for innovation and imagination. The old strategies are just not working anymore. The cutting edge in this field has moved beyond the patterns of the past and of the theories and fancies of the academics, I am afraid."

"Howard", he had continued, "there is a place for a man of your experience and training in the section. That place is just not as Director of Marketing."

Thompkins argument against experience reminded Howard of the contemptuous comment of his young colleague. "Experience is the schoolmaster of fools". The words rang, depressingly, in his head. From the beginning of their conversation Howard had increasingly felt like a plodding old dolt whom life had just raced by. This feeling, however, was quickly being displaced by the emotion of anger. He had served this company loyally for the whole of his working life and he had served it well. He had planned his career carefully, dedicated himself to the company's needs and tailored his life accordingly. And, now, his carefully acquired experience, skills and training were being carelessly tossed aside.

He posed the age question directly. Tompkins listened carefully to his question but brushed the issue quickly aside as irrelevant.

Howard left Thompkins office deeply dissatisfied and distressed. His career seemed in tatters. He sat at his desk and thumbed through the company manual on employment equity and harassment in the workplace. He had helped in drafting the policy but, at the time, had never even vaguely suspected that he himself would one day be thinking of laying a complaint under its provisions.

Case Study #3 Exercises

1. In your opinion is Howard a victim of harassment on the basis of age? Give reasons why or why not.

2. What is implied about age and experience in Thompkin's ideas concerning innovation, imagination and creativity? Are such ideas necessarily discriminatory?

3. Would Howard have a case under your organization's harassment policy? Why or why not?

4. What could Howard do to strengthen his case of discrimination and harassment?

Case Study #3 Discussion Notes

1. In your opinion is Howard a victim of harassment on the basis of age? Give reasons why or why not.

    Comments such as "getting rid of dead wood", "experience being the schoolmaster of fools" have been needling Howard and have been insensitive to a factor which he could not control.

    It is obvious that the comments caused Howard a great deal of stress and anxiety. It does not appear that he wanted to retire, such as many of colleagues had been forced to do. It would appear that the comments may have been designed to force Howard to retire on his own.

    When Howard was passed up for the promotion, Thompkins gave reasons related to conditions which Howard could not have controlled, such as his age. Thompkins seemed to be equating age with experience. Thompkins was discriminating on the basis of age, but he may not have been harassing.

2. What is implied about age and experience in Thompkins ideas concerning innovation, imagination and creativity? Are such ideas necessarily discriminatory?

    Thompkins assumes that youth equals innovation and imagination, but it has been found that there is no direct correlation between age and creativity. There are many elderly people who have developed creative ideas, while there have been many youthful people who have been very conservative towards progress and change.

    Such attitudes are definitely prejudicial. Since Thompkins was basing his decision not to promote Howard on that prejudicial attitude, it can be concluded that his actions are discriminatory.

3. Would Howard have a case under your organization's harassment policy? Why or why not?

4. What could Howard do to strengthen his case of discrimination and harassment?

    Howard could have been documenting each comment that he heard. He could note the names of the individuals who made the comments, the context in which they made the comments, and the names of other individuals who may have been present when those comments were made.

Howard should send a letter to Thompkins detailing the conclusions from their meeting. If Thompkins does not deny the conclusions, then Howard may use the letter as evidence of discrimination on Thompkins part. If Thompkins does deny the conclusions, then Thompkins will be forced to outline substantive reasons why another candidate was chosen over Howard for the position.

CASE STUDY #4

Martina had worked at the nursing home for the past eight years. She was a nurse's aid and provided personal hygiene services for the patients, shaving, bathing and otherwise caring for the personal needs of patients unable to care for themselves. She was good at her job, enjoyed good relations with her patients and got along well with her co-workers. She had received several awards and commendations for the quality of care she provided and for her dedication, above and beyond the ordinary call of duty, to improving the quality of life for residents at the home.

There was only one problem. Martina had tested positive for HIV, the virus that leads to A.I.D.S.

Martina had confided the distressing results of the test to one of her co-workers. The woman, a long-time friend, had been supportive but concerned and had urged Martina to alert the administration of the large company that ran the nursing home. Martina had refused. She was afraid of losing her job and only means of financial support and argued that the diagnosis was no business of the company's. She posed, she argued, no real or significant threat to the health of her patients.

Sylvia, Martina's friend and confidant strongly disagreed. Sylvia informed Martina that she felt duty bound to inform the administration of the condition of her friend's health. In this way Martina felt compelled to reveal her situation to the administrator of the facility.

From there, just as Martina had feared, the situation had snowballed to its seemingly inevitable conclusion.

Her supervisor had immediately insisted that she wear rubber gloves at all times when dealing with patients. There was no medical reason that she could discern for this measure as she was perfectly healthy except for carrying the much dreaded virus.

Knowledge of her condition spread rapidly through the institution. Her co-workers remained outwardly polite but most carefully and deliberately avoided physical and social contact. Surprisingly, perhaps, it was her patients who showed the least concern and demonstrated the most support. Several actually complained about her having to wear gloves while attending to their care.

During the ten days that followed, Martina found herself subjected to rumours regarding her personal life and to a number of embarrassing and distressing incidents. Several of her co-workers, for instance, had insisted on replacing the ceramic coffee mugs in the staff lounge with disposal paper cups. Pointedly, in Martina's presence, hygiene was cited as the reason for the change.

The support Martina received from her patients mattered little to the administration of the home and it found few echoes amongst her co-workers. Mr. Rand, the Director of the facility, found himself pressured to do something to resolve the situation.

On the one hand, the management of the central office of the company expressed grave concerns about continuing to employ Martina in the nursing home. It was obvious that they felt her continued presence in the facility threatened the public reputation and economic stability of the operation.

On the other hand, the non-unionized employees, Martina's co-workers had privately expressed their fears and concerns.

Rand, as he later testified at the Human Rights Inquiry, had originally hoped for a compromise. He had hoped to be able to retain Martina within the nursing home by re-assigning her to other duties away from the direct care of patients. This position, however, satisfied neither the central administration of the company nor the concerned among Martina's fellow workers.

Consequently, ten days after Martina's revelation of her condition, he summoned her to his office and, at the behest of head office, terminated her employment with the company. The usual severance pay plus an additional six weeks salary were the only compensation provided.

Rand explained to Martina that the company felt that they had to take this action in deference to the safety of the patients entrusted to their care.

Case Study #4 Exercises

1. Have Martina's rights been violated? How and for what reasons?

2. How would you have responded to Martina's admission that she carries HIV (a) as her co-worker and (b) as the manager of the nursing home. Give the reasons for your decision.

3. Does management, at all levels, have an educational responsibility and a leadership role to play in such a situation? If so what is that responsibility and role?

4. Should Martina have kept quiet about her condition or did she have a responsibility to inform her patients, co-workers and employers? Why or why not?

Case Study #4 Discussion Notes

1. Have Martina's rights been violated? How and for what reasons?

   Yes, Martina has lost her job due to perceptions that the disease can be spread through casual contact. Some staff are afraid to work with her and the company is afraid that negative public perceptions of the disease will hurt their business.

   Situations have been noted where a business discriminates due to the perception that its livelihood will suffer if it does not. Such situations have been noted in situations where the patrons of a bar insist that the owner remove certain "undesirables" or they will no longer frequent the bar. If the owner refused, it might just be likely that the "undesirables" will accept that bar and honour it with their business.

2. How would you have responded to Martina's admission that she carries HIV (a) as her co-worker and (b) as the manager of the nursing home. Give the reasons for your decision.

   A) As her coworker, one should make an effort to inform oneself of Martina's situation. Becoming aware of the means by which the disease is spread, the precautions that need to be taken, and the manner in which one can support a person with the disease are a few reasons that reading up and collecting information on the topic can be helpful.

   B) It would be the manager's responsibility to ensure that all staff and patients are aware of the disease and all its implications. Reading materials would be distributed and seminars arranged for all staff and patients to educate them on the issues of the disease. Overall, the manager should support the staff person and assist him/her to do the best possible job with the disease.

3. Does management, at all levels, have an educational responsibility and a leadership role to play in such a situation? If so what is that responsibility and role?

   Yes, the law has made employers responsible for the safety of their employees. Since the medical community has identified the detrimental effects of stress, employers are also responsible for the work environment. Such things include ensuring that employees do not suffer from harassment.

   The manager of the nursing home is responsible for ensuring that all employees are fairly treated and that their work environment is not detrimental or harmful. They must establish an environment which will encourage employees to be productive. The head office of the company and its senior executives are responsible for ensuring that proper policies and procedures are in place for the entire company and that all employees are aware of those policies and procedures. They must also provide support to their managers to effectively deal with instances of harassment.

4. Should Martina have kept quiet about her condition or did she have a responsibility to inform her patients, co-workers and employers? Why or why not?

There are a number of issues involved that must be considered. First, there is the argument that employers do not need to know anything that does not effect the performance of the employee. If the HIV virus does not develop into AIDS, then Martina should not tell the employer. However, there are arguments which say that if the HIV virus does develop into AIDS, then it is going to affect the employee's performance in terms of sick leave.

Second, as in Martina's situation, there are many prejudiced and ignorant people who will react from their fears rather than from facts. These people, such as Martina's co-workers who want her fired, are proposing discrimination in order to allay their own fears, not necessarily out of concern of the patients.

CASE STUDY #5

Carlo was deeply irritated. He knew he shouldn't be irritated but, somehow, that knowledge only served to increase his irritation. He didn't need problems like this and such problems seemed to be proliferating. He had a store to run and the recessionary economic pressures of the time were quite enough to contend with.

The country, he thought, is in the midst of its deepest economic recession in twenty years, the very future of the company is at stake, and I have to deal with a complaint about in-office jokes.

Patrick had just left his office. Patrick, the only openly gay employee in the store, was threatening to lay a complaint against several of his colleagues in the Furniture & Appliance Department. The guy should be glad to even have a job these days.

There had been, according to Patrick, a series of incidents. Carlo had little doubt that they had happened. In his mind the veracity of Patrick's complaint was not at issue. What was at issue was the seriousness of the allegations. Patrick seemed to have blown them out of proportion.

It seemed to Carlo that people had become excessively sensitive and cranky. No one, he thought angrily, used to get upset over jokes. People told jokes all the time about each other and only those devoid of any sense of humour got upset. You took such incidents in stride and gave as good back.

Patrick's complaint was two-fold. Two of his co-workers in the Furniture and Appliance Department, Reg and Andy, repeatedly told gay jokes. Patrick had failed to see the humor in these jokes and had told the two that he did not appreciate their attempts at humor.

Predictably, Carlo thought, Andy and Reg had been encouraged by this reaction on the part of Patrick. They had intended to tease him and they were delighted with the angry reaction they were eliciting. If Patrick had ignored them, Carlo thought angrily, if he had laughed at their silly jokes, that would have been the end of the matter. But, no, he had to take the whole matter with High Seriousness.

Carlo was sure that the second part of the complaint had arisen as a result of Patrick's behavior regarding the jokes of his colleagues. Certain derogatory remarks about Patrick's character and sex life had begun to appear on the walls of the men's public washroom in the Furniture and Appliance Department. There was no proof that Andy and Reg were the culprits.

Patrick claimed that he was being discriminated against as a gay person. He had told Carlo that he wanted something done about it. Carlo was sure that he was implying that if something wasn't done, then Patrick would do something more.

To Carlo's mind this and another related incident constituted the heart and importance of the affair concerning Patrick.

Apparently, angered by his co-workers' sense of humor, Patrick had treated the two to a lecture about the oppression of gays in the past. This lecture had been delivered publicly and during store hours. Luckily, Carlo thought, there didn't happen to be any customers present.

But what if there had been? How would the public react on overhearing such debates between the store's staff? Or, for that matter, how would they react if they connected the comments on the washroom walls with a clerk in the Furniture and Appliance Department?

Obviously, the matter had gone far enough. The productivity of his staff in the department was affected and the situation was clearly threatening to affect the good public image of the store.

The situation had to be resolved. He could hardly fire two of his best sales people for telling a few jokes. And, he had no proof that they were the authors of the comments on the washroom wall.

Clearly, he reasoned, the trouble is Patrick. He simply doesn't fit in and his presence in the department is creating unnecessary friction and a potential source of public embarrassment. Carlo smiled to himself as he reached for his phone and dialed the number for the head of the accounting department. Fortunately Patrick had a background in computer science. A transfer to the Accounting Department would solve the problem nicely for all concerned, he thought happily. At a single stroke, Patrick would be removed from the potentially embarrassing arena of contact with the public and from the presence of Reg and Andy. That will solve that problem, Carlo thought with relief.

Case Study #5 Exercises

1. How is Carlo treating Patrick's complaint? Why?

2. Was Patrick to blame for his lack of a sense of humor? Is Carlo correct in thinking that Patrick's reaction is the real source of the problem between him and his two colleagues? Give reasons for your reaction.

3. Should Carlo, as the manager of a department store, be concerned about public reaction to Patrick's open homosexuality? Why or why not?

4. What do you think of Carlo's proposed solution to the problem? Is it justified? Do you believe it will work? Why or why not? What would you have done in Carlo's place? State reasons.

Case Study #5 Discussion Notes

1. How is Carlo treating Patrick's complaint? Why?

   Carlo has trivialized Patrick's complaint.

   Carlo does not understand how jokes can be other than funny. He does not realize that some people make jokes about those things which they fear.

2. Is Carlo correct in thinking that Patrick's reaction is the real source of the problem between him and his two colleagues? Give reasons for your reaction.

   No. Carlo is wrong to think that Patrick is responsible for the problems. The behaviour in question originates with Reg and Andy. Therefore the problem also originates with them.

3. Should Carlo, as the manager of a department store, be concerned about public reaction to Patrick's open homosexuality? Why or why not?

   No. If certain members of the public are concerned about shopping at a store which employs gay people, then the manager should not be concerned about losing their business. If the business community refuses to tolerate prejudices of that sort, then eventually the remainder of society will not cater to prejudicial attitudes.

4. What do you think of Carlo's proposed solution to the problem? Is it justified? Do you believe it will work? Why or why not? What would you have done in Carlo's place? State reasons.

   Carlo's solution does not address the real problem. It is just a means for Carlo to get rid of the problem. The real problem is the attitudes of Reg and Andy. These two would probably find something about the next salesperson to "joke" about.

   Patrick is not likely to be very pleased with Carlo's solution. He may not accept it.

   Disciplinary actions should be taken against Reg and Andy to ensure that they do not harass any of the salespeople, including Patrick.

CASE STUDY #6

Martha sighed, the Halloween party had been an unmitigated disaster. Now, she had to deal with the consequences. She wondered if she should have foreseen the possibilities for disaster. Perhaps, she thought, I should have set guidelines for the costumes.

She sighed again and shook her head doubtfully. No, there were situations that were beyond foresight. When the staff party had been proposed it had seemed like a good idea; a fun way of building office morale.

The party had begun successfully enough. People began arriving dressed in the usual imaginative and unimaginative Halloween costumes. Ghosts and vampires mixed happily with Ninja Turtles, Egyptian mummies, astronauts and aliens.

The trouble, however, had begun in a sudden and dramatic fashion.

The door of the staff lounge had been ripped open and Madelaine Moffat strode into the room dressed as Adolph Hitler. Martha had to admit, the costume was good. The brown shirt, the mustache, red and black swastika arm band and polished riding boots rendered the young woman into a striking resemblance of the German tyrant and mass murderer. There were even those in the room who had laughed at the young woman's uncanny and somehow appropriate portrayal of the historic monster as she strode around the room loudly ranting about the Jews in a mock Germanic accent.

Martha remembered shaking off her initial shock. She had recovered quickly but, under the circumstances, no action could have been quick enough.

She had come up behind the ranting imitation Hitler and swept her forcibly off to the small kitchen that stood at one end of the lounge area.

She had closed the kitchen door and without saying a word had ripped off the young woman's false mustache. She was later told, by several helplessly amused individuals, that Madelaine's scream could be heard quite plainly in the outer room. She had then ripped off the swastika arm band with an equally silent but decisive display of force.

Martha had never known a cooler anger. She had quietly given the astonished Madelaine a firm twenty minute lecture on the totally unacceptable character of her behavior. The young woman had been sincerely astonished by this reaction. Initially, her attitude had been that it was all in fun and that no harm had been intended. When Martha had explained how such a costume and scene would look to her Jewish colleagues, Madelaine had been contrite. She had simply not seen her behavior from that perspective.

When they returned to the party, Madelaine shorn of most of her costume, Martha noticed that several of their Jewish colleagues had quietly left. Several others quickly made excuses and left, although they quietly accepted Madelaine's apologies.

This, however, was not to be the end of the evening's disasters. Just as 'Hitler' was beginning to be forgotten, two white members of the accounting department arrived dressed in black face as Clarence Thomas and Anita Hill.

The trouble came swiftly. Two of the firm's black employees approached the couple and told them in no uncertain terms what they thought of their costumes. They were backed up by several women who thought the costumes were not only racist but sexist in that they trivialized the subject of sexual harassment within the workplace.

The couple from accounting had refused to back down and the party ended when Howard, one of the protesting black employees had slugged Richard, the white accountant dressed as Clarence Thomas.

Martha had never faced a more serious nor a more complicated tangle of disciplinary problems.

In one way, Madelaine's offense seemed to her the most serious or at least the most flagrant. The young woman, however, had been guilty of nothing more than extreme thoughtlessness. She had not meant to offend, had been surprised that offense had been taken and had apologized contritely and sincerely.

The other case seemed less clear to Martha.

The couple from accounting had displayed, in her opinion, a remarkable degree of bad taste in choosing the subject of their costumes. Bad taste, however, was hardly a capital crime and it certainly, in her opinion, did not justify the violent reaction of Howard. Howard's violence had been inexcusable and she decided that her report would stress that fact.

Case Study #6 Exercises

1. Do you think that Martha is hypocritical in distinguishing between her reaction to Madelaine's costume and Howard's reaction to Richard's costume? Why or why not?

2. Is 'thoughtlessness' an acceptable excuse in such circumstances? Why or why not?

3. How would you compare the costumes of Madelaine and the couple from accounting with regard to sensitivity and social acceptability? Is the behavior of one less offensive than that of the other? Why? Why not?

4. Is Martha correct to judge Howard's reaction as unacceptable and that it should be stressed in the report? Can it be argued that violence can be provoked in a non-violent manner?

Case Study #6 Discussion Notes

1. Do you think that Martha is hypocritical in distinguishing between her reaction to Madelaine's costume and Howard's reaction to Richard's costume? Why or why not?

   While Martha did not actually strike Madelaine, she did use force to remove Madelaine's costume; hence Madelaine's scream. The only difference between the two situations is that Madelaine did not resist Martha's protest and action while Richard was resisting Howard's protest. Martha is being hypocritical.

2. Is 'thoughtlessness' an acceptable excuse in such circumstances? Why or why not?

   NO. One does not consider why they are being beat over the head with a stick, they only know that it hurts. In the same light, Madelaine's insensitivity towards the Jewish community is inexcusable because, regardless of her intentions, she still offended many Jewish people by her depiction of Hitler.

3. How would you compare the costumes of Madelaine and the couple from accounting with regard to sensitivity and social acceptability? Is the behavior of one less offensive than that of the other? Why? Why not?

   It cannot be determined whether one sensitivity is greater than another. The trials which the Jewish people suffered during Hitler's reign are horrible, but one cannot tell a Black American that they should be thankful for their situation as a result. Which is worse? Genocide or slavery? It likely depends on your perspective.

4. Is Martha correct to judge Howard's reaction as unacceptable and that it should be stressed in the report?

   NO. As we had discussed earlier, Martha is hypocritical in her judgment of Howard's reaction and her own reaction to Madelaine's costume. She may wish to identify Howard's reaction, but she should not stress it as it would bring in her own personal biases into the situation.

CASE STUDY #7

Ivan was slightly embarrassed. On his recommendation the Planning Committee had chosen Irene Williamson for the position of Community Liaison Officer. Now, he faced the rather awkward task of informing Marla Pritzker of their joint decision.

Ivan couldn't help feeling a certain degree of guilt. He struggled against the feeling that he had somehow betrayed Marla. It had been a tough decision, he reminded himself, and he ought to be able to live with it with a clear conscience. Both women had been about equally qualified for the position. However, he was sure that, under the circumstances, Ms. Williamson was the best person to do the job. This was no time to risk alienating the many benefactors of the Food Bank within the city's business community.

Still, it had been a very tough decision and he didn't look forward to disappointing Marla.

There was no doubting Marla's commitment to the Metro Food Bank. She had worked with the organization for the past three years. Without fail, she had come in twice a week for four hours. She had unpacked incoming boxes, sorted the goods and placed them on the shelves in the appropriate places. She had helped fill the orders of the people who used and depended upon the facility. She was a woman endowed with a warm and caring personality and she had done much to ease the pain of the desperate people who had been forced against their shame to draw upon the support of the Food Bank for the first time.

It was with a slight uneasiness that Ivan realized how these very qualities had counted *against* Marla in the Committee's decision to appoint Irene.

Perhaps their decision was unfair but, he argued to himself, they had to be realistic. He went over the factors that had decided the issue in his own mind and in those of the other Committee members.

Marla was a fine person and her commitment to the organization was unquestionable. She had proven herself through an unflagging loyalty and dedication. She was efficient and totally dependable. She just was not the right person for the post of Community Liaison Officer.

As a young and unemployed woman living on welfare she was not the person to approach and deal with the movers and shakers of the local business community on which the organization largely depended for its funds and donations. While Marla did have good communication skills, a person such as Marla would only serve to remind many of their biggest patrons of what they condemned in the country's social welfare system. Many of these business people objected to the extension of welfare benefits to healthy young people who happened to be unemployed. As employers, most refused to hire such unskilled, untrained and inexperienced young people but, at the same time, they objected to their collecting welfare. It was, Ivan thought, outrageously inconsistent and unfair of them. Nevertheless the organization had to be realistic.

That was the mentality of many amongst their largest patrons and they would have to deal with the world as it existed.

Irene Williamson was the wife of a local lawyer. She had a university education and had given up a career of her own in social work in order to raise three children in one of the best neighborhoods in the city. She knew many of the people the organization dealt with personally or by reputation. She spoke their language and knew how to best approach and present the case of the organization for aid.

No, Ivan reassured himself, they had made the right decision. It might not be fair but it was, realistically, the correct decision for the good of the organization.

Case Study #7 Exercises

1. Is Ivan justified in feeling guilty? Is he right in thinking that they had made the best decision "under the circumstances" and given the supposed realities of public opinion amongst the movers and shakers of the business community? Why or why not?

2. The fact that Marla is living on welfare was a key factor in deciding her suitability for the job of Community Liaison Officer for the Food Bank. Should this have been a factor? Give your reasons why or why not.

3. Is this a case of harassment? Why or why not?

4. Pretend you were on the Planning Committee that had to make the choice. What arguments would you advance (a) in favour and (b) against Marla's candidacy.

Case Study #7 Discussion Notes

1. Should Ivan feel guilty? Is he right in thinking that they had made the best decision "under the circumstances" and given the supposed realities of public opinion amongst the movers and shakers of the business community? Why or why not?

    Ivan is wrong for 'pandering' to attitudes which are discriminatory. He should not let those attitudes govern his decisions. While he may not want to appear controversial with those people, he should not allow their attitudes to figure in the decisions of the Food Bank.

2. The fact that Marla is living on welfare was a key factor in deciding her suitability for the job of Community Liaison Officer for the Food Bank. Should this have been a factor? Give your reasons why or why not.

    No. Source of Income does not determine whether someone is capable of doing a job or not. It most definitely was not in the qualifications for the Community Liaison Officer position. Ivan was very wrong of making that one of the criteria for the position.

3. Is this a case of harassment? Why or why not?

    No. It is a case of discrimination on the basis of income. It is not harassment because Marla is not being attacked for her economic position. Instead, she is being denied an opportunity.

4. Pretend you were on the Planning Committee that had to make the choice. What arguments would you advance (a) in favour and (b) against Marla's candidacy.

CASE STUDY #8

There were days when Jasbir loathed his new country. There were weeks and even months when he regretted leaving the familiar certainties of life at his birthplace; the largely-Sikh province of Punjab. In Canada, he thought, everything is a struggle.

Still, most of the time he enjoyed his new life and new land. Canada offered a kind of social security and economic opportunities that he had not even dreamt of at home in the Punjab. He had a good job as a loans officer with a small local credit union and he got along reasonably well with most of his colleagues. Occasionally, there had been little incidents of a racist nature but he had taken these in stride and dealt effectively with them.

What really irked Jasbir was the institutional discrimination he faced. The credit union seemed determinedly unwilling to bend in even the smallest ways to accommodate his particular cultural and religious background.

When he had first arrived in Canada, Jasbir had felt a tremendous sense of release and freedom. He was in a new land and he was prepared to lead a new life. He had, in the initial excitement of the adventure abandoned his Sikh religion and customs. He had decided that he would become as 'Canadian' as possible.

It was, in fairness to his employers, he thought, during this period that he had been hired to work for the credit union. Hence, he had begun working in the ordinary Canadian male attire of suit and tie. Except for a trim mustache, he had been clean shaven and without the turban and ceremonial dagger characteristic of the customary dress of more devout Sikhs.

His secular period had lasted nearly three years. Then, gradually, he had begun to feel the attraction of the old ways and beliefs. He had begun to feel that he was drifting away from the moorings of his personality and self. He had sought out members of the local Sikh community and begun the process of slowly rediscovering the cultural and religious roots of his identity. A year later, he had married into an orthodox Sikh family and sought formal re-admission to his wife's religious community. He had been accepted with understanding and encouragement. Now, he wished to live in complete accordance with his religion and bring up his children within its perameters.

The manager of the credit union where he worked had been polite but firmly unaccommodating. He was insistent that he had not hired a Sikh Loans Officer and that the turban and ceremonial dagger would be inappropriate dress within the context of the financial institution. They had few Sikh members, he had reminded Jasbir, and many Canadians had come to associate the traditional dress of the Sikhs with terrorism after the Air India bombings.

Jasbir felt that he now had to force the issue. Either his employer would have to accommodate the customs of his religion and culture or he would have to quit and find another form of employment more compatible with his beliefs and background. He intended to wear the turban and kirpan, or ceremonial dagger on his next workday. If fired, he would look to whatever civil protection the law offered.

Case Study #8 Exercises

1. Did Jasbir have the right to change his behavior and appearance after accepting the job in the guise of an 'ordinary Canadian'? Give the reasons for your answer.

2. Was Jasbir's first inclination, to abandon his religion and culture in favour of assimilation into the 'Canadian mainstream', right, wrong or neither right nor wrong? Give the reasons for your reply.

3. Imagine sitting on a human rights tribunal charged with settling a case arising out of these circumstances. Does the behaviour of the manager and the Credit Union constitute harassment in your opinion? Why or why not?

4. If it were demonstrated as fact that the Credit Union was losing business by employing a member of the Sikh community dressed in the traditional garb of that community, would the unaccommodating actions of the manager be justified? Why or why not?

Case Study #8 Discussion Notes

1. Did Jasbir have the right to change his behaviour and appearance after accepting the job in the guise of an 'ordinary Canadian'? Give the reasons for your answer.

   Of course. Canada is a country where freedom is valued, and that includes freedom to change one's appearance and behaviour if one so desires. The Credit Union cannot fire Jasbir on the basis of changing appearance because those changes do not affect his ability to do the job.

2. Was Jasbir's first inclination, to abandon his religion and culture in favour of assimilation into the 'Canadian mainstream', right, wrong or neither right nor wrong? Give the reasons for your reply.

   One may argue that Jasbir was neither right nor wrong because it was his own personal decision to conform to what was considered 'Canadian'. Had Jasbir felt external pressure to conform, as he is at the credit union, then it would be considered wrong.

3. Imagine sitting on a human rights tribunal charged with settling a case arising out of these circumstances. Does the behaviour of the manager and the Credit Union constitute harassment in your opinion? Why or why not?

   There is no doubt that systemic discrimination is taking place. Jasbir is being discriminated against on the basis of his religious dress; dress which can be formal and businesslike, but which is often considered un-businesslike by mainstream Canadian culture. In addition, a stereotype is at play with the manager worrying about members of credit union associating the bombing of Air India with all Sikhs.

   It can be argued that harassment is taking place with the implicit threat that Jasbir may be fired if he refuses to dress as a mainstream Canadian.

4. If it were demonstrated as fact that the Credit Union was losing business by employing a member of the Sikh community dressed in the traditional garb of that community, would the unaccommodating actions of the manager be justified? Why or why not?

   No. It is the responsibility of the credit union to demonstrate that it does not discriminate. If it is losing business due to prejudices in the community, than it must make efforts to educate its clientele about prejudice. *A business should not be allowed to break the law in order to improve its performance.*

CASE STUDY #9

At first Nancy had been excited and pleased, but now she felt almost cold and indifferent. Her six month trial term was almost up and her performance review had gone very well. But she still couldn't believe what had happened.

Six months ago, Nancy had received the first big chance in her career as an architect. The architectural firm had hired her for a six month trial term. At the end of the six months, the firm assesses her performance and determines whether a position is offered and, if so, what the bonus will be. Since the firm is one of the most successful, it has offered bonuses of up to $4000 for junior associates. Nancy could really use that money to pay off her debts from university.

About two weeks ago, Nancy had had a meeting with the Review Committee. The Associates on the committee had given her an excellent performance appraisal. Nancy had been elated and pleased at the time. She never expected that she would feel like this.

Then, late last week, a letter was delivered to her office inviting her for a meeting with a junior partner of the firm. She had been surprised that the meeting was with John Hoopla, a junior partner, as one of the senior partners usually conducted these meetings. She had been a little apprehensive about the meeting, but she had reassured herself that her performance appraisal had been very good and that she would be offered a position.

At the appointed time, she went to John's office. He was waiting for her, and invited her to sit in the chair across from his desk while he shut the door.

"So, today is the big day you've been waiting for. The last six months will all be determined in this one interview, eh Nancy?", said John.

Nancy just gave him a rather bland smile.

"I guess you were wondering why I'm conducting the interview instead of one of the Big Guys. Well, you know about the big meeting in the capital this weekend. Many of the Big Guys are away at the meeting, and they asked me to take care of this in the meantime."

"I trust that you're a bearer of good news.", said Nancy.

John chuckled. "Well Nancy, you know that your evaluation was excellent. The Big Guys had instructed me to inform you that you did just a fantastic job during these last six months. We are very happy with the work you do and we want you to stay with us."

"As you know Nancy, there is the question of a bonus for all the hard work you have done for us. Now, I have here a cheque that the Big Guys have signed, but they have left it blank. They instructed me to give you a bonus which I feel you deserve. Well I have thought the matter over very carefully and I have considered some things very carefully. I know that you really need this money, probably to pay off some of those school debts. I like you Nancy. You're bright, intelligent and hard-working. Above all, you are beautiful and I believe that you are hiding a beautiful body underneath those clothes."

Nancy was shocked, but John continued, "For a $500 bonus, you can take all your clothes off right now and let me see your beautiful body. For a $1000 bonus, you can spend tonight with me in a hotel room, and for $2000, you'll spend the weekend with me, Nancy. Now I suppose you want to know what you have to do for the big $4000 bonus. Well, I sure would like to have you with me at the conference at the capital next month. It is a whole week, and we could share a very comfortable hotel room together. So what do you say Nancy?"

"Well", said Nancy, "That's quite the proposal you have put to me, John. You've given me quite a few options there. You are right. I do need the money quite a bit. But, I'll need some time to think about which option I'll go for. But, in the meantime, I really don't believe that the Big Guys have left you with a blank signed cheque."

"No, really, they have.", replied John. "I have it right here."

"Let's see." asked Nancy.

John held up the cheque and Nancy took it and examined it closely. Sure enough, there was the signatures.

"Well, I guess you were right John. Thank you very much." Nancy folded the cheque in half, slipped into the front of her blouse, and walked out of the office, and down to the bank. She them filled out the cheque for $6000, and deposited it into her account.

She collapsed into her easy chair as soon as she got home, and reviewed the events of the day. While she was happy about the money, she wouldn't go through that again for any amount of money. But, she knew, she would never hear a word about this incident ever.

Case Study #9 Exercises

1. What is different about this case study from the previous case studies?

2. How did Nancy handle this situation so that it ended this way? Give the reasons for your reply.

3. Why was Nancy so sure at the end that she would never hear about this situation again?

4. What other options could Nancy have exercised?

Case Study #9 Discussion Notes

1. What is different about this case study from previous case studies?

   The harassment in this situation is blatant. Today, sexual harassers are likely to be more subtle due to the awareness of the problem.

   This situation had a "successful" ending for the victim.

   A most all harassment situations do not have a successful ending for the victim.

2. How did Nancy handle this situation so that it ended this way? Give the reasons for your reply.

   Nancy did not let the situation take control of her. She kept her head and dealt with the situation rationally.

   When John put the 'proposal' to her, Nancy immediately seemed to recognize the situation as a harassment situation, and immediately looked for the mistake that John had made, and how to turn the situation around.

   Nancy did not allow John to exercise power over her.

3. Why was Nancy so sure at the end that she would never hear about this situation again?

   John will most probably not tell his bosses the truth of how Nancy got the big bonus. Instead he will have to justify it on his own account, i.e., that he believes that her performance was so good that it warranted a larger-than-usual bonus.

4. What other options could Nancy have exercised?

   Nancy could have, first, approached John's boss, and then, if the results were unsatisfactory, approached the human rights commission with her complaint.

Part Seven

Harassment Policies:

Selected Public and Private Sector Examples

Part Seven: Harassment Policies: Selected Public and Private Sector Examples

The basic aim of corporate and institutional policies for dealing with harassment within the work environment is to define and encourage the paths of rational response while treating the emotional effects and consequences of such behaviour seriously and with sensitivity to the feelings of the abused worker.

Federal and provincial public services and crown corporations all have their own policies for defining and dealing with harassment in the workplace. Most of the larger private sector companies and organizations in the country have also implemented their own policies.

The following are brief descriptions of the essentials contained in a selection of public and private sector policies. These are offered as examples of how harassment can be defined and procedures instituted for the handling of complaints.

They are not offered, however, as *ideal* policies. They are *real* policies with flaws and imperfections as well as virtues. As such, they should not be copied blindly. They ought to be examined critically with an eye to improvement and to adaptation to the special and distinctive features of other organizations and workplaces.

A. PUBLIC SECTOR POLICIES

1. The Ontario Public Service*

A. Aims & Definitions

The most basic aims of the policy are to make it clear (a) that sexual harassment within the workplace is intolerable; (b) that all managers and employees have a joint responsibility for ensuring that their workplace is free from such behaviour and its consequences; and (c) to prevent and remedy the occurrence of such situations.

The policy defines *sexual harassment* in the terms of the *Ontario Human Rights Code*:

> engaging in a course of vexatious comment or conduct that is known or ought reasonably to be known to be unwelcome.

---

* **Human Resources Directives and Guidelines. Workplace Discrimination and Harassment Prevention. Directive of the Government of Ontario (March, 1992; Toronto)**

According to the Ontario policy, harassment may be one or a series of incidents in which an employee receives attention of a sexual nature which could reasonably be considered offensive, intimidating or hostile. The behaviour may be accompanied by the threat of penalty, such as the loss of a job, denial of promotion or of training opportunities. Or it may be activities which are directed at no one person in particular but which function to create a "poisoned environment" within the workplace. Sexual insults and jokes or the display of pornographic materials, for instance, are possible examples of the latter form of harassment behaviour under the terms of the policy.

A "poisoned environment" constitutes sexual harassment whether or not employees working within it choose to complain.

The policy gives the following specific examples of behaviours that clearly constitute sexual harassment under the policy:

* sexual assault;
* unwanted touching, patting and leering;
* sexually suggestive gestures;
* verbal threats or abuse;
* enquiries or comments about an individual's sex life.
* telephone calls with sexual overtones;
* sexual insults or jokes causing embarrassment;
* repeated unwanted social invitations;
* the displaying of pornographic or sexually sensitive material; &
* inappropriate comments about a person's physical appearance.

The policy clearly states that sexual harassment is not something that happens solely to women at the hands of men. While this is the most common form of sexual harassment, such behaviour can involve anyone in the workplace. Men may be harassed by women, men by men or women by other women. It can involve co-workers, management personnel, contract staff, clients, delivery people or members of the general public.

B. Procedures for Initiating & Handling Complaints

(1) Employees
The victim of such behaviour must realize that sexual harassment rarely goes away on its own; generally, it gets worse if the victim fails to act.

There are a number of options for employees to choose from in handling cases of sexual harassment.

* Informal Complaint under the Ontario Public Service Policy;

* Formal Complaint under the Ontario Public Service Policy;

* Grievances, Complaints to the Ontario Human Rights Commission;

* Use of the provisions of the Criminal Code;

* Launching a Civil Suit.

Victim of such behaviour ought to consider and choose the most appropriate and comfortable of these mechanisms for dealing with their concern. Victims are not limited to one option and may choose as many as they feel necessary.

The following are descriptions of the *Informal* and the *formal* complaint procedures internal to the Public Service policy.

Informal Complaints

Communicate your concerns about sexual harassment directly to the person(s) involved. This is often an effective and efficient way of dealing with the milder forms of behaviour on the harassment spectrum.

Tell the person(s) involved clearly that the behaviour in question is unwelcome and must stop. If this is done verbally, it is usually useful to have a witness present or to make a note of the conversation afterward. If you prefer to send a letter, it may be useful to keep a copy and proof that it was received (courier slip, registered mail receipt, etc).

It might be advisable to entertain the assistance of Ministry advisors and/or supervisors in the informal resolution of such incidents. However, if the informal complaint procedure is unsuccessful, your supervisor ***must*** discuss the issue with the Ministry advisor and/or investigator about the best way of resolving the matter.

Formal Complaints

Employees, for whatever reasons, may choose to forgo the informal process and immediately initiate a formal complaint.

Formal complaints may be filed within a reasonable time from the occurrence of the harassment incident. However, the sooner the complaint is filed, the easier it will be to establish facts and satisfactorily resolve the issue.

The formal complaint must be written and signed. It does *not* have to include a detailed account of the incident or incidents upon which it is based.

Such written complaints may be submitted to the ministry's advisor or investigator, an immediate supervisor, a supervisor or manager one level removed, or directly to the deputy minister, agency head or designate.

(2) Managers

Under the *Ontario Human Rights Code*, persons who have the authority to prevent or discourage harassment may be considered responsible for failing to exercise their authority in cases in which the complaints are not dealt with adequately or appropriately. Furthermore, the employer has a positive obligation to provide an harassment free working environment.

The first duty of the manager is, therefore, to prevent harassment. The best preventive measures are the following:

* Managers ought to show that they take the issue with the utmost seriousness.

* Managers ought to inspect the workplace with a view to detecting signs of harassment and of a poisoned environment.

* Managers shouldn't hesitate to approach employees when they suspect offenses.

Handling Informal Complaints

1: Deal with the issue promptly in consultation with the ministry advisor. Such problems generally get worse on their own. They do not tend to disappear.

2: Ensure that discussions of the case are held in private with no interruptions. At least initially, employees may be most comfortable being interviewed separately. Empathy and impartiality are called for. Remember that in some cases employees may be unaware that their behaviour was offensive.

3: Make notes in case you are required to testify at a later hearing.

4: Verify events whenever possible.

5: Discuss your conclusions with the parties involved.

Handling Formal Complaints

1: Once a complaint has been filed, inform the alleged harasser and give particulars of the charge.

2: Either the complainant or the alleged harasser may choose to have a union representative or lawyer present when filing a formal complaint and/or during meetings that they are required or entitled to attend. They may, at the discretion of management choose to have a co-worker attend.

3: If the complainant is a member of the bargaining unit, the formal complaint may be considered stage 1 of a sexual harassment grievance under the collective agreement.

2. Ontario Hydro

A. Aims & Definitions

The Ontario Hydro policy begins by asserting that:

> Every person has the right to equal treatment in employment without discrimination.

This statement is followed by a reminder that under the province's Human Rights Code, discrimination is defined as unequal treatment because of a person's race, ancestry, place of origin, color, ethnic origin, citizenship, creed, sex, sexual orientation, age, marital status, family status, record of offences or disability.

The policy explicitly links this definition of discrimination with harassment within the workplace.

> Every employee has the right to be free of harassment, for any of the above reasons, in the workplace.

The Ontario Hydro policy clearly defines harassment in terms of the *Ontario Human Rights Code* as "behaviour that is known or should reasonably be known to be unwelcome or offensive to an employee" or which "endangers an employee's job, undermines the performance of that job or threatens the economic livelihood of the employee".

B. Complaint Procedures for Individuals

Those within the workplace of Ontario Hydro who feel they have been discriminated against or harassed on any of the grounds specified in the *Ontario Human Rights Code* have two general options:

> (1) they can seek a fair and effective resolution by initiating Hydro's internal human rights complaint procedure;
>
> and/or
>
> (2) they may file a complaint externally with the *Ontario Human Rights Commission*.

Unfortunately, a third option exists and the company's policy can do nothing but openly discourage individuals from choosing it. That option, of course, is not to complain but to ignore or endure the unfair treatment and harassment. This is explicitly discouraged within the policy:

... because discrimination and harassment are assaults upon a person's dignity and can make an employee feel stressed, threatened and insecure.

C. Internal Complaint Resolution Procedure

Ontario Hydro's internal resolution procedure is designed specifically to address human rights complaints and to provide fast and effective resolutions. The emphasis of the process is on resolving the complaint as opposed to punishment. However, employees found to be discriminating against or harassing other employees, or supervisors who knowingly permit such behaviour, are subject to disciplinary action up to and including dismissal.

Those experiencing discrimination or harassment within the workplace ought to go for assistance to any of the following individuals:

their supervisor or next level supervisor or manager;

their Human Resources manager or officer;

the human rights manager;

staff in the Employment Equity Department;

their bargaining agent or representative.

Once a complaint is made, it is the duty of the complainant to co-operate fully with the subsequent investigation.

The company's internal resolution process can be used for complaints concerning either *direct* or *indirect* discrimination. *Direct discrimination* occurs when a person acts on his\her own against another person on any of the grounds prohibited in the province's *Human Rights Code*. *Indirect discrimination* exists when a person is acting upon the instructions of another.

The procedure has two components or pathways: (1) *Informal Complaints* and (2) *Formal Complaints*.

Path 1: If an employee feels that the situation can be appropriately resolved informally, then the process may begin by taking one or both of the following steps:

Step 1 Inform the offender in person or in writing that his\her behaviour is viewed as discriminatory or harassing, is unwelcome and ought to cease.

Step 2 Report the incident viewed as discriminatory or harassment to the supervisor, higher management or one of the designated contact people.

Under company policy, the supervisor or other individual who receives a complaint must:

* record the incident;

* investigate;

* provide a response to both parties involved in the complaint within fifteen days of its receipt.

Path 2: If the individual feels the informal process is inappropriate under the circumstances or if he/she is dissatisfied with the outcome of the informal process, then a formal, written complaint should be filed. The steps are as follows.

Step 1 The employee gives a written complaint, as soon as possible (but no more than six months) following the incident to his/her immediate supervisor, next level supervisor, human rights manager or Employment Equity Department Officers.

The complaint should contain the name(s) of the accused and the details of the discrimination or harassment. Details include: dates, times, places, witnesses and circumstances. The employee(s) making the complaint must sign it.

Step 2 The investigation begins once the complaint has been received. The investigation is conducted by someone trained in understanding human rights issues and legislation.

Step 3 The investigator will complete a report of the findings and suggest corrective action. The investigator's report will not normally take longer than two months to be concluded.

Step 4 The human rights manager will review the investigator's report and make recommendations to the line manager. The manager is responsible for taking corrective action where the investigation indicates that discrimination or harassment did occur.

Either the manager or the human rights manager is responsible for informing the employee who made the complaint of the investigation's findings and of the actions taken by management to resolve the situation.

Step 5 If the complainant is dissatisfied with the outcome of the process, a request may be made for a reconsideration of the case by the *Complaints Review Panel.* The following steps must be followed:

(5a) A written outline stating the reasons why a review is being requested. Copies go to the manager of the department concerned and the human rights manager.

(5b) A Complaints Review Panel is selected by the manager of Employment Equity and is composed of three managers outside the line organization of the employee requesting the review.

Step 6 The investigation and any additional information is reviewed by the panel. They are to make a decision and let both parties involved know of their decisions and the reasons for it within fifteen days of the review.

Decisions of the Complaints Review Panel are binding on management and must be implemented.

Step 7 If an employee experiencing harassment or discrimination is still not satisfied, a complaint may still be filed externally with the *Ontario Human Rights Commission.*

3. Manitoba Government Employee's Association (union)

A. Aims and Definitions

Harassment is against the law in Manitoba. Section 19 of the Human Rights Code specifically prohibits harassment. Section 5.1.3 of the MGEA Constitution outlines the MGEA's commitment to function free of discrimination and free from sexual harassment.

Harassment: any behaviour by any person that is directed at and is offensive to an individual. It encompasses but is not limited to harassment on the basis of race, sex, age, ethnicity, religion, sexual orientation, political belief/association/activity, and physical or mental disabilities.

Sexual Harassment: any sexual comments, gestures, or physical contact that are known or ought reasonably to be known to be unwelcome, objectionable or offensive, either on a one-time basis only or on a continuous basis. Sexual harassment is behaviour that is deliberate, unsolicited and unwanted. It is coercive and one-sided and both males and females can be victims of it.

Sexual harassment includes but is not limited to the following:

- unnecessary physical contact such as touching and patting
- suggestive remarks and other verbal abuse or threats
- leering at a persons body
- demanding sexual favours
- compromising invitations
- unwelcome remarks, jokes, innuendos or taunting
- displaying of pornographic, suggestive, offensive, or other derogatory pictures.
- condescension or paternalism which undermines self-respect
- physical assault
- sexual solicitation or advance made by a person in a position to confer, grant, deny or influence a benefit or advancement to the person; or
- reprisal or threat of reprisal for rejection of a sexual solicitation or advance, where reprisal is made or threatened by a person in a position to confer, grant, deny or influence a benefit or advancement to the person.

B. Background

Unions have taken the initiative in pressing for strong contractual and legislative measures to end the assault on working people's dignity. Sexual, racial, and other forms of harassment are not only workplace issues, but are also issues which surface throughout unions.

Human rights and solidarity are fundamental principles of the trade union movement. Harassment strikes at both. Trade unionists must work together to continue to protect the rights of all sisters and brothers. It is imperative to discard faulty stereotypes and learn to interact with mutual understanding and respect.

C. Policy Statement

Harassment of any kind is a serious offence. The MGEA will neither tolerate nor condone behaviour which is likely to undermine the dignity or self-esteem of an individual, or to create an intimidating or offensive environment. The MGEA is committed to providing a harassment free environment at all events.

D. Procedures

1. Talk to the Individual:

   If you as an MGEA member, staff person, or guest at an MGEA function feel that you are being harassed, you should let the individual know that his/her conduct is unacceptable and unwelcome.

2. Make a Complaint:

   If you choose to make a complaint of harassment, it should be directed to the President of the MGEA. If the President is not in attendance, the complaint should be directed to the person in charge of the event, who will bring it to the attention of the President immediately.

   It is important for people to voice their concerns while at the event so that appropriate measures can be taken immediately.

3. Investigation:

   All complaints of harassment will be investigated expeditiously and in a confidential manner.

4. Consequences:

   All complaints will be taken seriously. The appropriate level of discipline will be determined for substantiated complaints, which may include the removal of the harasser from the event.

   The President may determine further disciplinary action as necessary. Discipline would be in accordance with either the Staff Complaint Policy or Article 9 of the MGEA Constitution, whichever is appropriate.

B. PRIVATE SECTOR POLICIES

1. Bell Canada

A. Aims and Definitions

According to Bell Canada's policy, harassment means:

> any behaviour, typically repetitive in nature, which denies individuals their dignity and respect and which is offensive, embarrassing and/or humiliating.

Further, *sexual harassment* is distinguished as "any conduct, comment, gesture or contact of a sexual nature":

(a) that is likely to cause offence or humiliation to an employee; or

(b) that might, on reasonable grounds, be perceived by that employee as placing a condition of a sexual nature on employment or on any opportunity for training and promotion.

The general aim of the policy is to promote and provide a working environment for all Bell employees free of discriminatory practices and, especially, from all forms of harassment founded on grounds prohibited in Canadian human rights legislation.

The company commitment to a work place free of sexual harassment rests upon the conviction that every employee has the right to employment free from any conduct, comment, gesture or contact of a sexual nature that is likely to cause offense or humiliation or, on reasonable grounds, be perceived by the employee as placing a sexual condition on employment, training or promotional opportunities.

B. Procedures: Employee Initiated Complaints

Bell Canada's complaint procedure has been company policy since 1983.

Step 1: Employees of Bell Canada who feel they have a complaint covered under one of the ten grounds of discrimination defined by the *Canadian Human Rights Act* should, first of all, confront their harasser. Such employees should make their disapproval and/or unease known to their harasser immediately.

Step 2: If the harassment doesn't stop, employees should report their concern to their immediate supervisor.

If the employee feels that the problem cannot be reported to his\her immediate supervisor, then the report should be made to the next level of managerial authority, to the Personnel Counsellor (for managers and excluded non-management employees), to the Human Rights Coordinator or to the appropriate union representative (for bargaining unit employees).

Furthermore, the complainant of harassment ought to record the date of each incident as it occurs and note any relevant information (the nature of the remark, gesture or behaviour and the names of anyone present as witness).

Step 3: If the situation is not handled to the employee's satisfaction by his\her immediate supervisor, then the complainant should take the matter to another or higher managerial authority as outlined above.

Step 4: Notwithstanding the above procedure, employees who perceive they have a complaint covered under one of the ten grounds of discrimination defined by the *Canadian Human Rights Act* may, at any time, go directly to the *Canadian Human Rights Commission* with their complaint.

C. Human Rights Coordinators

Bell Canada has established the position of *Human Rights Coordinator* in order to provide a point of contact for employees with questions arising out of matters covered by the *Canadian Human Rights Act*.

The function of the Human Rights Coordinator is filled by selected Human Resources\Personnel Management staff. The Associate Director - Employment Equity can be contacted to determine the appropriate Human Rights Coordinator for a particular group. The Human Rights Coordinator conducts an investigation to determine all the facts of unresolved complaints referred to him/her.

D. Corporate Complaint Committee

A *Corporate Complaint Committee* will make recommendations on complaints involving discipline. The committee will act to ensure the resolution of complaints and the uniform treatment of employees.

The committee is authorized to meet as required under the chairmanship of the *Director -- Human Rights, Employment Equity and Staffing*. The other members of the committee will be: the Human Rights Coordinators(s) involved (or the appropriate personnel representative), a representative from the *Corporate Law Department* and appropriate representative(s) from other department(s) involved.

E. Penalties

Bell Canada considers harassment a serious offence. Under the company's policy, such behaviour can result in disciplinary action up to and including dismissal.

The company assures its employees that all complaints will be treated seriously and investigated thoroughly. The identity of the plaintiff, as well as information regarding any person or circumstances related to the complaint will remain confidential, except where disclosure is essential in the investigation and consequent disciplinary action.

Employees are actively encouraged to report such incidents and to seek assistance by following the steps outlined in the procedure. Under the terms of the company's policy, all Bell employees have a responsibility to play a role "in maintaining a workplace where individual rights and dignity are respected."

2. SaskTel

Personal Harassment Prevention Policy

A. Aims & Definitions

The aim of the policy is:

> To recognize the dignity and worth of every person and to provide for equitable rights and opportunities without discrimination.

SaskTel is committed to providing a work environment that is free from discrimination. Therefore, any physical or verbal conduct on the part of an employee towards another employee that amounts to discrimination or unfair treatment is strictly forbidden.

The *SaskTel* policy is a *personal harassment prevention policy. Harassment*, under the terms of this policy, is defined below.

> Harassment is any verbal or physical conduct which interferes with rights guaranteed by the Saskatchewan Human Rights Code and which is likely to cause offence or humiliation to any person, or to be perceived as placing a condition on employment, training, or promotion.

Under the policy, personal harassment of any kind is considered a serious offence subject to the full range of disciplinary penalties up to and including dismissal.

The policy draws distinction and defines both sexual harassment and racial harassment, with examples of each.

Sexual Harassment

Sexual harassment is a form of personal harassment and is defined as unwelcome conduct of a sexual nature that detrimentally affects the work environment or leads to adverse job-related consequences for the victims of the harassment.

This includes a person in authority making promises of favourable treatment in exchange for sexual favours (or conversely, retribution or punishment for failure to submit). It also includes verbal or physical conduct, on the part of managers or co-workers, that creates an intimidating, hostile, or offensive work environment or unreasonably interferes with an individual's job performance.

Sexual harassment may be found in one incident or a series of incidents. Harassment is always behaviour that is unsolicited and unwelcome. Some forms of sexual harassment include:

- leering; making sexually aggressive remarks.
- telling sexist jokes which embarrass others.
- making derogatory or degrading remarks directed towards members of one sex or one sexual preference group.
- deliberate and unsolicited physical contact that is unwanted, (e.g. touching, pinching, cornering, close body contact).
- making repeated offensive sexual flirtations, advances or propositions.
- displaying sexually offensive material (e.g. nude calendars, posters or printed material).
- solicitation involving threats or promises, or sexual/physical assault.

Racial harassment is also personal harassment and is defined as verbal or physical activity which has the effect of demeaning individuals on the basis of their racial backgrounds, and tends to define a relationship in which the parties are viewed as unequal simply on the basis of their race. (Race includes ancestry, place of origin, colour, ethnic origin, citizenship and creed). Examples of racial harassment include:

- making demeaning racial remarks, jokes, or innuendos about an employee, told directly to the employee or to other employees.
- making demeaning racial remarks, jokes, or innuendos about racial groups of which employees may be members, or which any employee of any race may find offensive.

- displaying racist, derogatory, or offensive pictures, graffiti, cartoons, or other materials.

B. Employee Procedures for Initiating Complaints

If you feel you are the subject of personal harassment, here are some guidelines for you:

Step 1: Make your disapproval and/or unease known to the harasser immediately.

Step 2: If the unfair treatment or the harassment does not stop after you have spoken to the harasser, speak to your immediate manager and then confirm your conversation in a letter. You may also speak with your union representative. If you are reluctant to speak with your immediate manager (or if the issue is not resolved to your satisfaction), speak with the next level of management or with any of the other parties identified in the "Complaint procedure" (i.e., e.g. Corporate Equity Director, or Manager, Industrial Relations).

Step 3: Send a copy of your letter to your department manager or next level of management (if appropriate) and to the Corporate Equity Director.

Step 4: If there is more than one incident, keep a written record of dates, times, the nature of the behaviour, and any witnesses.

Step 5: Ensure that the harasser is advised that you have taken the above steps.

C. Managerial Procedures for Handling Complaints

Management has the responsibility to ensure that the acts of managers are in no way discriminatory or encroach upon the rights of employees. Therefore, management has the duty to respond immediately to complaints and follow these steps:

Step 1: Respond immediately. Interview both the complainant and the alleged harasser as soon as possible. Also interview any witnesses.

Step 2: Document the situation accurately and completely.

Step 3: Render a decision as soon as possible and advise the parties of any action to be taken. Consultation with Employment Equity and Industrial Relations <u>is required</u> in situations where disciplinary measures are being considered. If higher authority is required to make a decision (higher management levels or other appropriate departments), forward all material as soon as possible to the appropriate authority and advise both parties of the action taken.

Step 4: Ensure that all information concerning the case is kept confidential and not placed on the complainant's personal files. Files may be forwarded to Employment Equity for storage.

Step 5: Monitor the situation periodically for the next 6 months to ensure that nothing untoward has happened following the investigation and resolution. (Retaliation against a complainant or witness is considered an offense and will be considered misconduct).

NOTE: Managers should work toward a discrimination-free work place, by communicating SaskTel's policy, ensuring all employees are aware of the issues of harassment, and by encouraging complainants to come forward to resolve difficulties.

All employees of the corporation (management and non-management) are responsible for contributing to a work environment that is free from personal harassment. Respect for the dignity and worth of an individual is a corporate value which all employees are expected to uphold.

All instances of taunting, teasing, joke-telling, etc. are not necessarily considered harassment. The line is crossed where the conduct amounts to an unwarranted intrusion upon an individual's dignity.

Sometimes we don't realize how our actions or words are interpreted. Some basic guidelines for contributing to the prevention of harassment in the work place are below:

- When in doubt, don't say it' don't do it.
- When in doubt, ask if it's all right.
- If a behaviour is unwanted, stop the behaviour.
- Don't assume that friendliness equals sexual interest.
- Don't assume that lack of comment means that people aren't offended.
- If you see others engaging in offensive behaviour, suggest they stop.

3. Petro Canada

A. Aims and Definitions

The policy at Petro Canada is focused specifically on the phenomenon of *sexual harassment*. The stated aim of the policy is three-fold, providing:

(1) a workplace conducive to productivity;

(2) a workplace in which the dignity of the individual is respected; and

(3) a workplace free from sexual harassment or the threat of sexual harassment.

Under the terms of its policy, the company assumes full responsibility for ensuring that its workplace comes up to these standards. It also promises that the company will take:

> such disciplinary action as it deems appropriate against any person under its direction who subjects any employee to sexual harassment.

The Petro Canada policy defines sexual harassment as:

> any conduct, comment, gesture or contact of a sexual nature that is likely to cause offense or humiliation to an employee, or that might, on reasonable grounds, be perceived by that employee as placing a condition of a sexual nature on employment, work assignment, or on any opportunity for training or promotion.

This definition is followed by a list of specific examples of forms of behaviour that are to be regarded as sexual harassment under the terms of this definition. They include:

* Unwelcome remarks, jokes, innuendos or taunting of a sexual nature about a person's body, attire, age, marital status;
* unwelcome or intimidating invitations or requests with sexual overtones whether indirect or explicit;
* leering or other gestures;
* unwelcome physical contact such as touching, patting or pinching;

* unwelcome display of objects or pictures of a sexual nature;

* sexual advances, requests for sexual favours, or other verbal or physical conduct of a sexual nature:

(a) when submission to such conduct is made explicitly or implicitly a term or condition of employment;

(b) when submission to or rejection of such conduct is used as the basis for decisions affecting an employee's employment, promotion or movement within the organization;

(c) when such conduct has the purpose or effect of humiliating an individual or substantially interfering with an employee's work performance or in creating an intimidating, hostile or offensive work environment.

B. Roles & Responsibilities

The provision of a working environment free of sexual harassment is a basic responsibility of management under the terms of the company's policy. Specifically, management is charged with the following duties and obligations:

(1) management must take whatever steps necessary to ensure that all employees are informed of the company's policy on sexual harassment;

(2) management must provide clarification of what constitutes sexual harassment behaviour.

(3) management must inform all employees of the exact procedures in place for the pursuit and handling of sexual harassment cases;

(4) management has the responsibility of initiating complaints, without waiting for the victims of such behaviour to complain, when sexual harassment is known to be taking place. To do otherwise, constitutes misconduct on the part of the manager;

(5) management is obligated to act when complaints are received.

C. Procedures for Initiating & Handling Complaints

(1) Employees

Step 1 : When an employee feels that sexual harassment has taken place, he/she should advise the offender(s) that the behaviour is unacceptable and unwelcome. A written record of dates, times, witnesses and the nature of the behaviour ought to be kept.

Step 2: The complainant should report the alleged offence to his\her supervisor, the Director of Human Resources, the Human Resources designate or, in the case of employees covered by a collective agreement, the grievance procedure should be followed.

(2) Managers

Step 1: Upon receipt of a formal complaint of sexual harassment, the supervisor or manager must inform the Director of Human Resources.

Step 2: Inform the harasser, supervisor and complainant, in writing, that an investigation is to take place.

Step 3: Conduct an investigation with Human Resources.

Step 4: Inform, in writing, the complainant and the alleged harasser of the outcome of the investigation.

Note: Petro Canada has just developed a comprehensive workplace harassment policy to deal with all forms of harassment.

Part Eight

Legislation Concerning Harassment

Part Eight: Legislation Concerning Harassment

The federal, provincial and territorial levels of government have all enacted human and civil rights legislation that deals with harassment. The following are brief sketches outlining the provisions related to harassment in each of these jurisdictions.

1. BRITISH COLUMBIA

Section 8, *Human Rights Act*, British Columbia, prohibits discrimination in employment on the basis of "race, colour, ancestry, place of origin, political belief, religion, marital status, physical or mental disability, sex or age . . . or because of . . . conviction for a criminal or summary conviction charge . . . unrelated to employment . . . or . . . intended employment". Sexual and other harassment charges are handled under this section of the *Act*.

The investigation and settlement of such complaints is the responsibility of the *British Columbia Council of Human Rights*.

Under the B.C. *Human Rights Act*, employers and organizations are responsible for the actions and behaviors of their employees. The obligation to prevent and quickly stop sexual and other forms of harassment within the workplace rests with employers and those in positions of managerial and supervisory authority.

If sexual harassment occurs, the employer may be held responsible or partially responsible and ordered to pay compensation for wages or salary lost or expenses incurred as a result. An additional payment, not exceeding $2,000.00 may be levied as an award to the victim of harassment.

The Act is administered by:

British Columbia Council of Human Rights
2nd Floor, 844 Courtney Street
Victoria, B.C.
V8W 1C4

(604) 387-3710

2. ALBERTA

In Alberta, sexual and other forms of harassment are handled under the provisions of the *Individual's Rights Protection Act*. The investigation and arbitration of cases is the responsibility of the *Alberta Human Rights Commission*. The Alberta Human Rights Commission defines sexual harassment as:

> . . . unwanted sexual advances, unwanted requests for sexual favours, and other unwanted verbal or physical conduct of a sexual nature . . .

Such behaviour constitutes sexual harassment when:

> . . . submission to such conduct is made either explicitly a term of condition of an individual's employment, tenancy, or the receipt of service
>
> or when
>
> . . . submission to or rejection of such conduct by an individual demonstrably affects that individual's employment, tenancy, or receipt of service.

Under Alberta legislation, employers are responsible for maintaining a working environment that is free from the taint of sexual harassment for *all* employees. This responsibility applies not only in the case of supervisor/subordinate relations but also between co-workers of equal or relatively equal status.

Supervisors who fail to effectively deal with a complaint regarding harassment may be liable under the provisions of the *Individual's Rights Protection Act*. Prompt and appropriate action on the part of supervisors and employers is mandatory.

The Act safeguards the equality rights of all Albertans and, generally, prohibits discrimination on the grounds of "race, colour, ancestry or place of origin, religious beliefs, gender or because of a physical or mental disability. It also prohibits discrimination in employment on the basis of age (18 and over) and marital status.

The Act is primacy legislation. It overrules other provincial laws that may be in conflict with it.

Forms of harassment other than sexual may well be covered under the provisions of the legislation.

The Act is administered by:

The Alberta Human Rights Commission
10808-99th Avenue, Room 805
Edmonton, Alberta
T5K 0G5

1-800-432-1838

3. SASKATCHEWAN

The Saskatchewan Human Rights Code prohibits all forms of discrimination in the employment arena (except in cases of clearly defined and reasonable occupational qualifications). Sexual and other forms of harassment within the workplace are covered under the provisions of the Code.

Under this legislation it is the responsibility of the employer to provide a discrimination- and harassment-free working environment. Harassment is clearly identified as discriminatory behaviour.

Whether they are aware of the harassment or not, employers are responsible for the occurrence of such actions and behaviours within their businesses.

Management and supervisory personnel who fail to deal effectively and promptly with such situations may also be liable under the Code.

Employers and responsible supervisors may also be held accountable for harassment by non-supervisory staff in certain circumstances. For instance, if an employee is harassed by another employee and if employers or supervisors know but do not take reasonable steps to intervene, they may be held wholly or partially responsible.

The *Saskatchewan Human Rights Code* is administered by the *Saskatchewan Human Rights Commission*:

> Saskatchewan Human Rights Commission
> 8th Floor, Sturdy Stone Building
> 112-3rd Ave. North
> Saskatoon, Saskatchewan
> S7K 2H6
>
> (306) 933-5952

4. MANITOBA

The *Manitoba Human Rights Code* prohibits discrimination based on the following grounds:

> . . . physical or mental disability, actual or perceived, ancestry (including colour and perceived race), nationality, ethnic origin, religion, age, sex, pregnancy, sexual orientation, marital or family status, source of income and political belief.

The Code explicitly identifies harassment [section 19 (1)] as discriminatory. As Section 19 (2) clearly states, the provisions of the Code apply to all forms of harassment and not solely to sexual harassment.

Section 19 (1b) makes it clear that anyone who is privy to an act of harassment within the workplace must take reasonable steps to terminate the behaviour or be held responsible under the terms of the legislation.

Section 19 (2) defines harassment as follows:

> (a) a course of abusive and unwelcome conduct or comment undertaken or made on the basis of any of the characteristics defined above.
>
> (b) a series of objectionable and unwelcome sexual solicitations or advances; or
>
> (c) a sexual solicitation or advance made by a person who is in a position to confer any benefit on, or deny any benefit to, the recipient of the solicitation or advance, if the person making the solicitation or advance knows or ought reasonably to know that it is unwelcome; or
>
> (d) a reprisal or threat of reprisal for rejecting a sexual solicitation or advance.

It should also be noted that the *Manitoba Human Rights Code* explicitly prohibits discriminatory behaviours, actions and comments directed towards persons with A.I.D.S. or H.I.V. Infection. Employment and pre-employment enquiries or medical testing related to an individual's H.I.V. status are illegal unless an employer can establish that being free from the virus is a reasonable requirement or qualification for the job or position in question.

Harassment of people infected or thought to be infected with the H.I.V. or A.I.D.S. is clearly prohibited under the provisions of the Code.

The Code is administered by:

> The Manitoba Human Rights Commission
> 301, 259 Portage Avenue
> Winnipeg, Manitoba
> R3B 2A9
>
> 1-800-282-8069

5. ONTARIO

The Ontario Human Rights Code prohibits discrimination in employment on the following grounds:

> . . . race, ancestry, place of origin, colour, ethnic origin, citizenship, creed (religion), sex (including pregnancy), sexual orientation, handicap (physical or mental disability), age (between 18 and 65 years in employment), marital status, family status, the receipt of public assistance and record of offences.

The Code explicitly forbids harassment within the workplace. Harassment is defined as:

> . . . a course of bothersome comment or conduct that is known or ought to be known to be unwelcome. Sexual solicitations or advances made by a person who can grant or deny a benefit to the person solicited are also prohibited.

The Code recognizes racial slurs, jokes and racially motivated acts of harassment as discriminatory behaviour. Under the provisions of the Code it is an offence to communicate slurs and jokes of a racial nature and everyone is guaranteed the right to a working environment free from such harassment.

The legislation also includes provisions covering "poisoned environments". Individual rights may be violated under the terms of the Code even in cases where racial slurs and/or actions are not directed against an individual. The display of racist, derogatory or offensive pictures, graffiti or materials, demeaning racial remarks, jokes or innuendos and remarks about a racial group in the presence of any individual, not necessarily a member of the group in question, can constitute breeches of the Code.

Employers are responsible for the discriminatory acts of their employees. Moreover, supervisors and managerial personnel are liable under the Code for failing to prevent, discourage or stop harassment. Prosecution for failing to exercise authority with regard to harassment is possible.

The Code provides redress for three common types of sexual harassment.

> 1. A course of vexatious comment or conduct that is either known or ought reasonably to be known to be offensive and unwelcome.
>
> 2. Sexual advance or solicitation by persons in a position to grant or deny a benefit. Such behaviour contravenes the Code when the person making the advance or solicitation knows or ought reasonably to know that such behaviour is unwelcome.

3. Threats or reprisals from persons in a position to grant a benefit against an individual who has rejected or refused a sexual advance or solicitation.

The *Ontario Human Rights Code* is administered by the province's *Human Rights Commission*:

Human Rights Commission
400 University Avenue
Toronto, Ontario
M7A 2R9

(416) 965-8837

6. QUEBEC

The *Quebec Charter of Human Rights and Freedoms* was adopted in 1975 with the following fundamental aims:

(1) to promote the rights of individuals, of groups and of the community in Quebec;

(2) to encourage respect towards all and the accountability of each individual for others and for the common weal;

(3) to help individuals and groups to attain recognition of their rights and to exercise their rights;

(4) to guard against discrimination and exploitation.

The Charter explicitly prohibits harassment. The relevant sections read as follows:

10. Every person has a right to full and equal recognition and exercise of his/her human rights and freedoms, without distinction, exclusion or preference based on race, colour, sex, pregnancy, sexual orientation, civil status, age except as provided by law, religion, political convictions, language, ethnic or national origin, social condition, a handicap or the use of any means to palliate a handicap.

> Discrimination exists where such a distinction, exclusion or preference has the effect of nullifying such right.
>
> 10.1 No person may harass a person on the basis of any ground mentioned in section 10.

Within the meaning of the Charter, harassment means the *repetition* of words, acts or gestures of a vexatious or contemptuous nature with regard to a person or group of persons on the basis of the grounds identified above.

Further, all employers are responsible for acts of harassment that occur within their workplaces. They are liable if they do not intervene as soon as they learn of such situations.

The *Commission des droits de la personne du Quebec* is the agency charged with the administration of the investigation and arbitration of charges and complaints filed under the provisions of the Charter. Address:

Commission des droits de la personne du Quebec
360, rue St.Jacques
Montreal, Quebec
H2Y 1P5

(514) 873-5146

7. NEW BRUNSWICK

In the province of New Brunswick the *Human Rights Act* prohibits discrimination on the grounds of race, religion, colour, nationality, place or origin, ancestry, age, family or marital status, and physical or mental disability.

A study of the Act entitled, *Towards a World Family*, was concluded and released to the public in November, 1990. This study strongly recommended that sexual orientation be added to the list of prohibited grounds. A committee of the legislature has been established to study the report and make recommendations to the government. Public hearings on the *Towards a World Family* study were held in February, 1991, but the committee has yet to make its report to government.

While harassment is not covered by the New Brunswick legislation, sexual harassment is prohibited. Many cases involving sexual orientation are, thus, covered under this aspect of the Act.

The *New Brunswick Human Rights Act* is administered by the *New Brunswick Human Rights Commission*, Fredericton:

New Brunswick Human Rights Commission
103 Church Street
P.O. Box 6000
Fredericton, New Brunswick
E3B 1B0

(506) 453-2301

8. NOVA SCOTIA

Nova Scotia's *Human Rights Act* has recently (1991) undergone significant amendments. The amended Act prohibits discrimination in all facets of public life within the province.

Currently, discrimination in employment is prohibited on the grounds of:

> . . . age, race, colour, religion, creed, sex, sexual orientation, physical or mental disability, an irrational fear of contracting an illness or disease, ethnic, national or aboriginal origin, family status, marital status, source of income, political belief, affiliation or activity and an individual's association with another individual or class of individuals having any of the above characteristics.

The amended Act attempts to define more clearly what constitutes sexual harassment and discrimination based on pregnancy.

The Act is administered under the authority of the *Nova Scotia Human Rights Commission*:

Nova Scotia Human Rights Commission
P.O.Box 2221
Halifax, Nova Scotia
B3J 3C4

(902)424-4622

9. PRINCE EDWARD ISLAND

The intention of the *Prince Edward Island Human Rights Act* is to ensure that all persons in the province have equal rights with regard to employment and other areas of public life.

The Act prohibits discrimination in employment on the following grounds:

> . . . race, religion, creed, colour, sex, marital status, ethnic or national origin, age, physical or mental handicap and political belief.

In terms of the Act, sexual harassment is understood to be a form of discrimination on the basis of sex. Such harassment must be (1) of a sexual nature (which is understood to include inappropriate comments); (2) unwelcome; and (3) have a negative impact upon the victim's employment situation.

The province's *Human Rights Act* is currently being interpreted in light of recent decisions on the nature of harassment made in judgments by the *Supreme Court of Canada* and by the *Ontario Board of Inquiry* and other human rights commissions across the country.

The Act is administered by:

> The Prince Edward Island
> Human Rights Commission
> 3 Queen Street
> P.O.Box 2000
> Charlottetown, Prince Edward Island
> C1A 7N8
>
> (902) 368-4180

10. NEWFOUNDLAND & LABRADOR

The *Human Rights Code* prohibits discrimination in employment on the basis of the following:

> . . . race, religion, religious creed, sex (including pregnancy), marital status, physical or mental disability, political opinion, colour or ethnic, national or social origin or age (between 19 and 65). The only exceptions

are for reasons of sound occupational qualification and the burden of proof rests with the employer.

Harassment is explicitly identified under the terms of the Code as discriminatory behaviour and is generally prohibited on the grounds of race, religion, sex, mental and physical disability, etc.

Sexual solicitation by persons in positions to grant and deny benefits or advancement is prohibited in cases where the person knows or reasonably ought to know that the advances or solicitations are unwelcome.

Persons with the authority to prevent, discourage or stop harassment are responsible under the provisions of the Code for making reasonable efforts to do so. Complainants may name the company as a party to the complaint as well as the actual harasser(s).

The Code is administered under the authority of the *Newfoundland Human Rights Commission*:

Newfoundland Human Rights Commission
6th Floor, 345-47 Duckworth Street
P.O.Box 8700
St.John's, Newfoundland
A1B 4J6

(709) 576-5812

11. YUKON

Section 13 of the *Yukon Human Rights Act* prohibits harassment on any of the grounds generally prohibited under the provisions of the legislation. These are:

ancestry (including colour and race);

national origin;

ethnic or linguistic background or origin;

religion, creed, religious belief, religious association or religious activity;

age;

sex (including pregnancy and pregnancy related conditions);

sexual orientation;

physical or mental disability

criminal charges or criminal record;

political belief, political association or political activity;

marital or family status;

actual or assumed association with other individuals or groups whose identity or membership is determined by any of the above grounds.

The *Yukon Human Rights Act* is administered under the authority of the *Yukon Human Rights Commission.*

12. THE NORTHWEST TERRITORIES

The Northwest Territories does not have its own human rights legislation. Human rights issues within the Territories fall under the jurisdiction of the *Canadian Human Rights Act* (described below **in the section on federal legislation).**

13. CANADA: FEDERAL LEGISLATION

The Canadian Human Rights Act prohibits discrimination on ten grounds:

race,

national or ethnic origin,

colour,

religion,

age,

sex,

marital status,

family status,

pardoned conviction,

disability.

The Act specifically provides that discrimination based on pregnancy or childbirth is prohibited.

Disability means any existing or previous mental or physical disability, and includes disfigurement and dependence on alcohol or a drug.

Section 13.1 of the Act defines harassment as a discriminatory practice in matters of employment and such actions grounded on any of the ten protected categories is prohibited. Sexual harassment is explicitly identified as a prohibited ground of discrimination under the Act.

Protection from harassment extends to acts occurring away from the workplace as well as those that may occur within the work environment.

Harassment behaviour, under the provisions of the *Canadian Human Rights Act* may be:

verbal,

physical,

deliberate,

unsolicited,

unwelcome,

one incident or a series of incidents.

For a practice to be deemed harassment, it must be reasonably shown as:

* a term or condition of employment (including availability or continuation of work, promotion or training opportunities);

* an influence on decisions regarding such matters;

* an interference with job performance;

* as humiliating, insulting or intimidating to an individual.

The employer is responsible for maintaining a non-discriminatory work environment. This means that employers are, ultimately, responsible for acts of harassment committed by employees or agents. The employer has an obligation under the Act to exercise reasonable diligence in the *prevention* and prompt *termination* of such actions.

Derogatory comments, taunts, jokes, slurs, threats, teasing comments about race, colour, national or ethnic origin, or about the adornments, dress, customs associated with cultural and religious backgrounds are all considered as harassment under the Act.

In a recent decision, the *Supreme Court of Canada* adopted a definition of sexual discrimination that included:

> . . . practices or attitudes which have the effect of limiting the condition of employment of, or the employment opportunities available to a person, on the basis of a characteristic related to gender.

The court, in adopting this definition, made it clear that sexual harassment within the workplace was to be considered discrimination on the basis of sex. In the same decision, the Chief Justice of the Court defined sexual harassment as:

> unwelcome conduct of a sexual nature that detrimentally affects the work environment or leads to adverse job-related consequences for the victims of the harassment.

Responsibility for the administration of the *Canadian Human Rights Act* lies with:

The Canadian Human Rights Commission
320 Queen Street
Place de Ville, Tower A
Ottawa, Ontario
K1A 1E1

(613) 995-1151

Part Nine

Resources

Part Nine: Resources

A. VIDEOS

A Class Divided. 1985, 60 minutes. (Topic: a powerful lesson about the nature of prejudice and the effects of discrimination and harassment by a Grade 3 teacher. In 1970 an American TV network made a documentary, *Eye of the Storm*, on the effects of the method. *A Class Divided* updates the lesson in a blend of film from the original documentary and a reunion of the original grade 3 class of 1970).

Behind the Mask. My Partners, My People, 1989, 30 minutes. (Topic: negative stereotyping of Native people in education and society at large.

Beyond The Open Door. 30 minutes. (Topic: Equity issues in the workplace. A documentary format. Individuals who have suffered discrimination and harassment talk about their experiences).

Confrontation Games. 3/4 in. 60 minutes. (Topic: attitudes and perceptions).

Courting Equality. VHS. (Available from the Alberta Human Rights Commission, 102 1333 8 St. SW., Calgary, Alberta. T2R 1M6).

Doing What's Right. Saskatchewan Human Rights Commission, 1986, 30 minutes. (Topic: provisions of the Sask. Human Rights Code).

Facing Racism. VHS. 16 minutes, 50 seconds. (Topic: Racism in the Workplace).

Gift of Freedom. 1/2 in. 50 minutes. (Topic: cases under Charter of Rights and Freedoms).

Human Rights, Human Wrongs. Canadian Living Magazine, 1988, 30 minutes. (Topic: the disturbing story of discrimination in Canada; the causes and consequences of discrimination and ways of fighting discrimination).

No one Ever Complained. VHS. (Available from the Alberta Human Rights Commission, Calgary).

Opportunity for All. 1/2 in. 30 minutes. (Topic: prejudice and discrimination in the workplace).

Say No to Racism. Regina Public School Board, 1987, 30 minutes. (Topic: a project of race relations conducted in Regina public schools.

Sexual Harassment in The Workplace. Labour Canada, 1988, 20 minutes. (Topic: what is sexual harassment? How does human rights law deal with it? How can it be discouraged in the workplace?).

Silent Crisis. 1/2 & 3/4. 30 minutes. (Topic: sexual harassment).

Taking Action. VHS. 27 minutes. (Topic: Petro Canada's programme on sexual harassment).

The Charter and You -- The Canadian Charter of Rights & Freedoms. 3/4in. 59 minutes.

Universal Declaration of Human Rights -- Amnesty International. 1/2 in. 21 minutes.

Workplace Hustle. Clark Communications, 1980, 33 minutes. (Topic: sexual harassment in the workplace. Moderated by Ed. Asner, it has a combination of narrative and dramatic scenes).

B. BOOKS & ARTICLES

Baldrige, Letitia & Judith Martin ('Miss Manners'), "A Sexual Etiquette Guide", *Time Magazine*, October 21, 1991, p. 30.

Bergman, Brian, "Women in Fear", *Maclean's Magazine*, November 11, 1991, pp.26-32.

Canadian Press, "First Sikh Officer to Wear Turban says: 'It's a Dream Come True'", *Halifax Chronicle Herald*, May 13, 1991, p.A4.

Conway, Sheelagh, "Campus Critique Leaves Women on Margins", *Globe & Mail*, October 24, 1991, p.A19.

Cox, Kevin, "New Brunswick Gays want Laws to Protect Rights", *Globe & Mail*, November 17, 1990, p.A5.

Duffy, Peter, "Has AIDS Made Gays Society's New Lepers?", *Halifax Chronicle Herald*, December 12, 1990, p. A2.

Edelstein, Barry, "All the World's a Senate Confirmation Hearing", *Globe & Mail* (reprinted from: *The New Republic*), November 2, 1991, p.D5.

Ehrenreich, Barbara, "Women Would Have Known", *Time Magazine*, October 21, 1991, p.33.

Erskine, Bruce, "Police Commission to Look at Job Equity", *Halifax Chronicle Herald*, July 25, 1991, p.A1.

French, Orland, "Sex Wars Still Rage on Campus", *Globe & Mail*, November 11, 1989, pp.D1-2.

Galen, Michele, "Sexual Harassment: Out of the Shadows", *Business Week*, October 28, 1991, pp.30-35.

Gibbs, Nancy, "Office Crimes", *Time Magazine*, October 21, 1991, pp.26-30.

Goleman, Daniel, "Harassment: Not About Sex but Power", *Globe & Mail*, October 26, 1991, p.D10.

Gowen, Jim, "CFB Halifax Officials Probe Allegations of Harassment", *Halifax Chronicle Herald*, December 28, 1990, p.A3.

Grant, Donald, "Mastering Technology to Give Some Freedom to the Physically Disabled", *Globe & Mail*, September 1, 1990, p.D4.

Hays, Arthur S., "How the Courts Define Harassment", *The Wall Street Journal*, October 11, 1991, p.B1.

Hughes, Susan, "Women's Struggle", *Halifax Chronicle Herald*, February 19, 1991, p.B13.

------., "Banks Discard Old Stereotypes", *Halifax Chronicle Herald*, February 19, 1991, p.B13.

______., "Bank Examines Women's Barriers", *Halifax Chronicle Herald*, February 19, 1991, p.B13.

------., "Pay Disparity Irks Nursing Assistants", *Halifax Chronicle Herald*, January 4, 1991, p.A3.

Kramer, Michael, "Shame on Them All", *Time Magazine*, October 21, 1991, pp.24-25.

LeBlanc, Susan, "The Fight for Nova Scotia Blacks", *Halifax Chronicle Herald*, October 26, 1991, p.C1.

______., & Rob Gorham, "New Vision for Nova Scotia Blacks", *Halifax Chronicle Herald*, July 6, 1991, p.B1.

______., "Racial Tensions a Symptom of National Malaise", *Halifax Chronicle Herald*, July 25, 1991, p.A3.

------., "Arab-Canadians Face Harassment", *Halifax Chronicle Herald*, February 14, 1991, p. A3.

Lethbridge, Gail, "N.S. Barristers' Society to Study Gender Equality", *Halifax Chronicle Herald*, July 6, 1991, p.D22.

------., "War Against Women", *Halifax Chronicle Herald*, December 1, 1990, p.B1.

Lubin, Joann S., "Companies Try a Variety of Approaches To Halt Sexual Harassment on the Job", *The Wall Street Journal*, October 11, 1991, p.B1.

MacDonald, Cindy, "Educational Opportunities For Disabled 'Few and Far Between'", *Halifax Chronicle Herald*, November 13, 1990, p.A10.

MacKillop, Malcolm J., "Right of Refusal: Progressive Employers Recognize the Need for a Corporate Policy on Sexual Harassment", *Human Resources Professional*, October 1991, pp.6-7.

McBride, John & Tom Morron, *Look Again: The Process of Prejudice and Discrimination*, Vancouver: Commcept Publishers Ltd., 1977.

Meek, Jim, "Racism a Fact of Life in Our Town, Mr. Mayor", *Halifax Chronicle Herald*, July 24, 1991, p.A6.

Mills, Rob, "Sexist Language", *Halifax Chronicle Herald*, February 15, 1990, p.B1.

Noble, Kimberley, "Being a Bad Sport about Harassment", *Globe & Mail*, November 29, 1991, p.A20.

Pennar, Karen, "Women are still Paid the Wages of Discrimination", *Business Week*, October 28, 1991, p.35.

Poirier, Patricia, "Quebec Rights Watchdog Riles Minorities", *Globe & Mail*, November 13, 1991.

Popular Educational Resources, *Detecting Prejudice: A Handbook for You on Discrimination in Visual Materials*, Toronto: Williams-Wallace Productions, 1979.

Ross, Oakland, "True Office Romance", *Globe & Mail*, November 2, 1991, p.D1.

Scott, Ian, "Women Jump Hurdles to Business Success", *Halifax Chronicle Herald*, October 24, 1989, p.B1.

Smith, Geoffrey, "Consciousness-Raising Among 'Plain Old White Boys'", *Business Week*, October 28, 1991, p.32.

Stephens, Laurie, "Ontario Firms Implementing Pay Equity Legislation", *Halifax Chronicle Herald*, September 19, 1989, p.A11.

Sullivan, Lynne, "10 Commandments on Sexual Harassment", *Globe & Mail*, November 4, 1991, p.B4.

Sword, Pam, "Canada Said Ahead on Integrating Disabled Students into Schools", *Halifax Chronicle Herald*, July 21, 1989, p. A30.

______., "Women's Contributions do not Make History Books", *Halifax Chronicle Herald*, October 4, 1989, p.A17.

Taylor, Kate, "Love Among the Desks: It doesn't Have to be Harassment", *Globe & Mail*, November 8, 1991, p.A19.

Taylor, Wilkie, "Blacks, Micmacs Denied Equal Opportunity in Pictou Schools -- Exchange Students", *Halifax Chronicle Herald*, November 22, 1991, p.A7.

Tibbetts, Janice, "Female Professors Face Discrimination", *Halifax Chronicle Herald*, January 19, 1991, p.C2.

Unsigned, "Disabled Woman Compensated for Abuse", *Halifax Chronicle Herald*, January 30, 1991, p.D11.

Unsigned Editorial, "Not Funny, but Offensive", *Halifax Chronicle Herald*, February 14, 1990, p.A6.

______., "Review Finds It's a Tough World for Canadian Women", *Halifax Chronicle Herald*, February 18, 1991, p.A6.

Waddell, Christopher, "Most Think Women's Chances Limited, But Oppose Affirmative Action", (*Globe & Mail\CBC News Poll*), *Globe & Mail*, February 12, 1990, p.A10.

White, Jack, "The Stereotypes of Race", *Time Magazine*, October 21, 1991, p.32.

Wolfe, Morris, "Artful Dodgers: How Much Progress Has Ontario's Art College Made Towards Employment Equity?", *Saturday Night*, December, 1990, p.15&ff.

York, Geoffrey, "Gay Officers Live in Limbo", *Globe & Mail*, November 6, 1991, p.A9.

Part Ten

Index

Part Ten: Index

A

B

C

D

E

F

G

H

The
McDonald Series

TO ORDER CALL

1-800-665-4854

Leading Resource Guides on Diversity

NAME:____________________ SIGNATURE:____________________

TITLE:____________________ DEPARTMENT:____________________

ORGANIZATION:____________________

ADDRESS:____________________ CITY:____________________

PROVINCE:____________________ POSTAL CODE:____________________

PHONE: (   ) ____________________ FAX: (   ) ____________________

Set / Titles		Price	Quantity	Discounts	Totals
Set #1:	**Four of the titles below**	**$85.00**			
	Managing Diversity	$25.00			
	OR Guide de la gestion de la Diversité	$25.00			
	Designated Group Retention	$25.00			
	Communicating Across Cultures	$20.00			
	Racism, Sexism & Homophobism: Harassment	$32.00			
Set #2:	**Two Titles below**	**$25.00**			
	Interviewing Aboriginal Peoples	$20.00			
	Summary of Aboriginal Issues Today	$12.00			
	Teacher's Guide to Summary of Aboriginal Issues Today	$5.50			
The McDonald Quarterly	**1 year sub.**	**$80.00**			
	2 year sub.	**$150.00**			

* Books (except McDonald Quarterly) are PST exempt in Manitoba

GST	
PST	
sub-total	
Shipping & Handling	
TOTAL	

BUY SETS AND SAVE UP TO 22% !!

DISCOUNTS

BUY 10 or more of a publication and receive............................20% discount off the total order
BUY Set #1 and receive..20% discount off the regular price of The McDonald Quarterly
BUY Set #1 and Set #2 and receive...25% discount off the regular price of The McDonald Quarterly
BUY 20 Summary of Aboriginal Issues Today and receive ....One FREE copy of The Teacher's Guide to the Summary
Charitable groups (# required) & Public Libraries receive.............50% discount off the regular price of The McDonald Quarterly

PAYMENT (✓): ☐ **Please invoice** ☐ **Cheque attached**

Send your order to:

Cross Cultural Communications International, Inc.
200-275 Portage Avenue
Winnipeg, Manitoba, Canada, R3B 2B3

HAR2P